THE DAY EVIL DIES

CLIFFORD GOLDSTEIN

REVIEW AND HERALD® PUBLISHING ASSOCIATION
HAGERSTOWN, MD 21740

The author assumes full responsibility for the accuracy of
all facts and quotations as cited in this book.
The author is indebted to certain concepts and descriptions
in Ellen G. White, *The Great Controversy*.

This book was
Edited by Gerald Wheeler
Copyedited by Jocelyn Fay and James Cavil
Designed by Willie Duke
Electronic make-up by Shirley M. Bolivar
Cover design by GenesisDesign/Bryan Gray
Typeset: 11/13 Bembo

PRINTED IN U.S.A.

03 02 01 00 99   5 4 3 2 1

R&H Cataloging Service
Goldstein, Clifford Ralph, 1955-
    The day evil dies.

    1. Second Advent.   2. Eschatology.   3. End of the
world.   I. Title.

                        236

ISBN 0-8280-1456-6

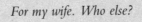

For my wife. Who else?

CONTENTS

"I HAVE SEEN BEAUTIFUL THINGS!"

Romanian Jew Richard Wurmbrand survived the Nazis but only barely the Communists, who imprisoned him for 14 years because of his Christian faith. Of all the jailhouse brutalities he faced, one of the worst was the refrigerator cell, a room coated with frost and ice.

"Prison doctors," he wrote, "would watch through an opening until they saw symptoms of freezing to death, then they would give a warning and guards would rush in to take us out and make us warm. When we were finally warmed, we would immediately be put back in the ice-box cells to freeze—over and over again! Thawing out, then freezing to within just one minute or two of death, then being thawed out again. It continued endlessly. Even today sometimes I can't bear to open a refrigerator."[1]

The Communist captors, Wurmbrand wrote, sealed Christians for hours in boxes barely bigger than themselves. The guards drove sharp nails into the boxes from every side. As long as the prisoners stood perfectly still, they were OK, "but when we became fatigued and swayed with tiredness, the nails would go into our bodies. If we moved or twitched a muscle—there were the horrible nails."[2]

However traumatic those years, Wurmbrand saw incredible examples of courage by those who—beaten, battered, and abused—remained undaunted, undiminished, and undefeated in their faith, even to death.

Though the authorities forbid preaching to other prisoners, for example, and severely punished those who violated the rule—many Christians did so anyway. One prisoner was witnessing when the guards hauled him away. After a beating, they dumped him, bloody and bruised, back on the cell floor. "Slowly," wrote Wurmbrand, "he picked his battered body up, painfully straightening his clothing, and said, 'Now, brethren, where did I leave off when I was interrupted?'"[3]

After being tortured with red-hot pokers, after being locked in a room with starving rats, even after being made to stand up for two weeks straight—a pastor named Florescu refused to reveal the names of other Christian believers. The Communists then brought his 14-year-old son into the prison and beat him up in front of his father. As Florescu cried out, the child screamed, "Father, don't do me the injustice to have a traitor as a parent. Withstand! If they kill me, I will die with the words 'Jesus and my fatherland.'"[4] Enraged, the Communists killed the child, the boy's young blood splattering over the cell wall as the father helplessly watched.

The Communists had sentenced another Christian to die. Before the execution they allowed him to meet with his wife, but in the presence of a secret police officer. *"You must know that I die loving those who kill me,"* the condemned man told her. *"They don't know what they do and my last request to you is to love them too. Don't have bitterness in your heart because they kill your loved one. We will meet in heaven."*[5]

How did Wurmbrand know what happened? Because the secret police officer—after hearing the condemned man's words to his spouse—became a Christian and was himself thrown in prison for his faith!

"I have seen," wrote Richard Wurmbrand, "beautiful things!"[6]

Not every Christian, of course, has seen such "beautiful things." But all have, to some degree, experienced the struggle to maintain faith, truth, and obedience in a world opposed to all three. One does not need to be chained in a Marxist dungeon to know the struggle, the controversy, between good and evil, right and wrong, faith and unbelief that rages around and in us. Indeed, often the fiercest and most consequential struggles unfold—not in dramatic spectacles that could be glamorized in a Hollywood script—but in the quivering folds of the human heart.

"Two souls, alas," wrote the German poet Goethe, "are lodged within my breast, and struggle there for undivided reign." Malcolm Muggeridge described the "human drama" as unfolding an "obvious dichotomy" between two forces: "One is the Devil," he wrote, "and the other God."[7] Expressing the same idea, American jurist Oliver Wendell Holmes wrote: "We are all soldiers in a great campaign, the details of which are veiled from us."

However we personally frame the terms of this "great campaign" or understand the issues involved, the battle still rages, in one form or another everywhere and with everyone. Only two ways out of it exist—never to be born, or to die.

An article in *The New Yorker* told about a Christian woman in South America who kept on singing hymns and "strange evangelical songs" while soldiers raped her. Even when they shot her in the chest, she kept on singing, "a bit weaker than before," the article said, "but still singing." The soldiers watched, stupefied. "Then they had grown tired of the game and shot her again, and she sang still, and their wonder began to turn to fear—until finally they unsheathed their machetes and hacked her through the neck, and at last the singing stopped."[8]

For the most of us, the struggle for faith, dignity, or obedience isn't as violent, as stark, or so *instantly* consequential. The battle is, nevertheless, just as real, just as profound, and ultimately just as consequential even if its manifestations often appear more subtle. We are, as it were, on a seesaw, tilting in one direction or another between right and wrong, good and evil, faith and unbelief. Who can pass even a single day without making moral choices or having the conscience twiddled, prodded, or tweaked? Though not usually confronted by extremes, we're always tipping, or vacillating, in small steps toward them. And, as we slowly approach the extremes, the far edges, they don't seem so distant or extreme after all.

Through no choice of our own, we exist in a

world in which good and evil, right and wrong, law and lawlessness, dignity and dishonor, faith and unbelief vie for supremacy. Every day our thoughts, actions, and words place us on one side or another in this great spiritual conflict. However complicated its manifestations appear, however blurry, fuzzy, and gray our moral options, choices, and decisions seem—there are only two sides, only two choices: good and evil, truth and error, right and wrong. As with life and death, there's no middle ground, however much we fool ourselves in thinking that's where we stand.

"I call heaven and earth to record this day against you, that I have set before you life and death, blessing and cursing: therefore choose life, that both thou and thy seed may live" (Deuteronomy 30:19).

And that's ultimately our option—life or death. Not to choose one is to wind up with the other; to choose neither is, really, to choose death. But the Lord beckons us to "choose life"—and life is found in Jesus Christ, His Son. "He that hath the Son hath life; and he that hath not the Son of God hath not life" (1 John 5:12).

It's a choice with eternal consequences—because life and death are, literally, forever.

Someone once asked Billy Graham if he were an optimist or a pessimist.

"I am an optimist," he answered. "I've read the last page of the Bible."[9]

He ought to be. And so should any other repenting, confessing soul who has made the hopes, the promises, the surety of those last pages their own—for the Word of God reveals that at the end of this great controversy, good wins over evil, faith over unbelief, truth over error, and Christ over Satan. Unlike most other battles in which the outcome is almost always in question, we not only know beforehand the winning side—we're guaranteed (if we choose) to rejoice in the "spoils."

"And I saw a new heaven and a new earth: for the first heaven and the first earth were passed away; and there was no more sea. And I John saw the holy city, new Jerusalem, coming down from God out of heaven, prepared as a bride adorned for her husband. And I heard a great voice out of heaven saying, Behold, the tabernacle of God is with men, and he will dwell with them, and they shall be his people, and God himself shall be with them, and be their God. And God shall wipe away all tears from their eyes; and there shall be no more death, neither sorrow, nor crying, neither shall there be any more pain: for the former things are passed away. And he that sat upon the throne said, Behold, I make all things new" (Revelation 21:1-5).

John's words aren't poetry, fancy metaphor, or whimsical imagery—they are the Lord Himself promising us a personal place in a new existence, one far more real and enduring than the fleeting, crippled world waxing old before our eyes and crumbling beneath our toes.

However much realistic and secular minds may mock the notion of heaven and eternity in bliss as just human myths desperately seeking to make the here and now more tolerable, God's Word time and again clearly and unambiguously promises us a reality too wonderful for reason and rationality alone ever to comprehend. The Lord Himself vows to give us an existence purified and cleansed of every trace of sin. He holds out to us a world in which the pitiful and humiliating absurdities of human contradictions will pass away into something so precious, so comforting, so happy that everything we have suffered here will fade into nothing but a barely remembered nightmare.

Until then we struggle with the hard questions. Why does a loving Lord in heaven allow suffering on earth? What is the nature of this great controversy between Christ and Satan, good and evil? How will it climax? Why did God allow sin? How does an omnipotent God ultimately vindicate His name and honor amid a world quivering in unreconciled pain? What can Christian history teach us about the Christian future? What role will the churches play, for good or evil, in the final events that lead to Christ's return? What relevance, if any, does God's law still have?

These are some of the questions that this book—relying upon inspired writings—seeks to answer. Outlining the themes of the great conflict between Christ and Satan, it begins with the earliest days of the Christian church, follows it up through the Protestant Reformation to the religious world today, and ends with the grand climax at the end of the ages—all in an attempt to unravel these questions, however partial and incomplete the answers may be, if for no other reason than that only partial answers have been given for now.

Meanwhile, "what we cannot speak about we must pass over in silence."[10]

[1] Richard Wurmbrand, *Tortured for Christ* (Glendale, Calif.: Diane Books, 1967), pp. 36, 37.

[2] *Ibid.,* p. 37.

[3] *Ibid.,* p. 43.

[4] *Ibid.,* p. 36.

[5] *Ibid.,* p. 45.

[6] *Ibid.,* p. 43.

[7] Malcolm Muggeridge, *Jesus Rediscovered* (1969), p. 100.

[8] Mark Danner, *The New Yorker,* Dec. 6, 1993, p. 87.

[9] Billy Graham, *Angels: God's Secret Agents* (Dallas: Word Publishers, 1986), p. 149.

[10] Ludwig Wittgenstein, *Tractus Logico-Philosophicus* (Atlantic Highlands, N.J.: Humanities Press International, 1993), p. 74.

CHAPTER TWO

FROM JERUSALEM TO WITTENBERG

B efore His death Jesus stood on Mount Olivet and uttered ancient Jerusalem's epitaph: "If thou hadst known, even thou, at least in this thy day, the things which belong unto thy peace! but now they are hid from thine eyes. For the days shall come upon thee, that thine enemies shall cast a trench about thee, and compass thee round, and keep thee in on every side, and shall lay thee even with the ground, and thy children within thee; and they shall not leave in thee one stone upon another; because thou knewest not the time of thy visitation" (Luke 19:42-44).

Christ's lament was not in anticipation of Calvary and the horrible darkness that would engulf Him when He offered Himself as the sacrifice for the world's sin. Rather He cried for the doomed inhabitants of Jerusalem and for the glorious Temple that, though then gleaming brightly in the sun like a polished jewel, would soon incinerate like a stick of parched wood.

Forty years later Roman legions under Titus consummated a siege of the city that brought unbelievable misery inside its crumbling walls. Famine and pestilence left thousands dead with no graves but the bellies of scavaging birds. Starving parents battled their own offspring over everything semidigestible (even pigeon droppings). According to the historian Josephus, "the upper rooms were full of women and children that were dying by famine; and the lanes of the city were full of the dead bodies of the aged; the children also and the young men wandered about the marketplaces like shadows, all swelled with famine, and fell down dead wheresoever their misery seized them." [1]

No wonder Jesus wept.

Yet Christ's tears on Mount Olivet weren't just for Jerusalem, but for a world hardened in unbelief, rebellion, and sin—a world that one day will meet the retributive judgments of a God who for thousands of years has painfully watched His creation degraded, defiled, and damned through sin and disobedience. The destruction of Jerusalem was but a faint shadow, a localized symbol, of the final, universal, and just destruction of a planet that has rejected both the mercy and the law of the Lord—a rebellion that has resulted in human history being one long shrill shriek uttered by those reaping not just the consequences of their own sins but of the sins of others.

Just when we think humanity can't get more inhuman, it always does. And just when we conclude that the defiance of God's law can't get any more blatant, the human race sinks to new levels of depravity. Whether it is a father purposely infecting his infant son with AIDS in order to avoid paying child support,

16

or people murdering a woman in late pregnancy to steal the fetus from her womb, or children 13 and 14 shooting up their schools—these are all just the latest manifestations of the heartsickening crimes that have blemished each century. They are crimes that will ultimately be answered for in the great day of judgment, when the Lord will come to claim His own while bringing justice to those who have spurned the mercy, forgiveness, and healing He has offered to all.

Jerusalem, unfortunately, never accepted that mercy, forgiveness, and healing, all so freely and expensively offered—and so it reaped the natural results that rebellion brings. Sadly, the world is no more open to God now than was Jerusalem 2,000 years ago. It too will reap the same bitter harvest.

Not all the inhabitants of Jerusalem, however, perished in the siege. The followers of Christ, heeding His warnings, fled to safety miles away. But their troubles were hardly over. Satan, using pagan Rome as his weapon, unleashed the furies of hell against the Christians. Stripped of their possessions and driven from their homes, they were charged with bringing pestilence, earthquakes, and famine upon the empire. Often before rancorous crowds whose winesaturated breath polluted the air above amphitheaters, Christians were crucified, burned alive, or fed to lions and vicious dogs.

"Mobs subjected them to insults, blows, the stocks, imprisonment, plundering, the arena, fire in the iron chair, stonings. Brought before the forum by the authorities, the accused Christians were publicly examined and subjected to torture. Some heathen servants, fearing torture, told of Thyestean feasts and Oedipodean incest among the Christians, thus arousing the populace to new heights of rage. Sanctus, after being burned over the tender parts of his body with red-hot brass plates, was thrown into prison and retortured in the same manner a few days later. Bishop Pothinus, though ninety and ill, was kicked and beaten before the governor and hurled into a dungeon where he died two days later. The virgin Blandina, a slave, mangled and broken in torture, was finally gored by a bull. Corpses of martyrs choked the streets. Dogs feasted. After some days' exposure, the mutilated bodies were burned and the ashes dumped in the Rhone River to make resurrection more difficult."[2]

Yet the very persecution intended to destroy the Christian church actually caused it to grow. The more intense the wrath, the more determined Christians were to be faithful, even to death.

Thus what violence, torture, and force could not attain, trickery and flattery did instead. Rather than continuing to attack the church, Satan made it comfortable, respectable, and secure. The world soon accepted Christians and, more important (as Satan planned), Christians became *accepting of the world.* Because being a Christian now cost nothing, pagans joined en masse, adopting some biblical doctrines while retaining pagan hearts. Idolaters changed merely their objects of veneration from images of pagan deities to images of Christ, Mary, or the saints. The forms, customs, holidays, and superstitions of pagan temples quietly dressed themselves in Christian garb.

As it left hovels and catacombs and entered courts and palaces, the church increasingly laid aside the humility of Christ and the apostles for the pomp and majesty of pagans and their priests. With the "conversion" of Emperor Constantine in the fourth century and the rapid growth of the church, it seemed—at least on the surface—that Christianity had triumphed.

Yet it was paganism, not the faith of Christ, that had won. Pagan Rome continued, dressed in the decor, if not the spirit and teachings, of Christ. The bishop of Rome took over where Caesar had left off as the tiara simply replaced the crown. As seventeenth-century British political scientist Thomas Hobbes said: "If a man consider the original of this great ecclesiastical dominion, he will easily perceive that the papacy is no other than the ghost of the deceased Roman Empire, sitting crowned upon the grave thereof."[3]

Such paganization of Christianity, however, did not take the God of heaven by surprise. Long before, the apostle Paul warned that Christ would not return "except there come a falling away first, and that man of sin be revealed, the son of perdition; who opposeth and exalteth himself above all that is called God, or that is worshipped; so that he as God sitteth in the temple of God, shewing himself that he is God" (1 Thessalonians 2:3, 4). The early Christian church unmistakably fulfilled the apostle's warning. Pagan concepts distorted and even replaced biblical teaching and practice.

The doctrine, for instance, that places the bishop

of Rome as the head of Christ's church has no scriptural support. The most fundamental of all biblical teaching, salvation by faith in Christ alone, vanished within a vast and intricate system of works, penances, and pilgrimages. The Christian doctrine of salvation degenerated to the point that people thought that through indulgences they could obtain forgiveness from the penalty of sin, or that money dropped in church coffers could release family and friends from purgatory. The pagan day of the sun, Sunday, replaced the biblical seventh-day Sabbath, a change with no scriptural justification. In fact, the prophet Daniel had warned of a power that would "think to change times and laws" (Daniel 7:25). False teachings such as that of purgatory or limbo crept into Christian theology. The ordinance of the Lord's Supper mutated into the sacrifice of the Mass, a sacrament that, at its core, teaches that the church has the power to create God.

John Charles Ryle, bishop of Liverpool, described the condition of the church in England prior to the Protestant Reformation: "To the clergy, as a rule, religion was the merest form and scarcely deserved to be called Christianity. The immense majority of the clergy did little more than say masses and offer up pretended sacrifices, repeat Latin prayers, and chant Latin hymns—which, of course, the people could not understand—hear confessions, grant absolutions, give extreme unction, and take money to get dead people out of purgatory. . . . At Reading Abbey, in Berkshire, the following things (among many others) were exhibited by the monks on great occasions, and most religiously honored by the people: an angel with one wing, the spearhead that pierced our Saviour's side, two pieces of the holy cross, Saint James's hand, Saint Philip's stole, a bone of Mary Magdalene, and a bone of Salome."[4]

Through the long centuries, corruption, superstition, avarice, debauchery, and greed had become so prevalent in the medieval church that even a devout Catholic such as Dante (1265-1321) had consigned pope after pope into the deepest pits of hell. Rome, in turn, displayed little tolerance for dissent, and often Catholics who spoke out against the church faced the wrath of Satan himself.

Among the faithful Catholics who opposed the false doctrines and corruptions of the papacy was John Wycliffe. The fourteenth-century English Reformer dared to confront the church hierarchy with the truths of God's Word. Besides protesting the degrading influence of the mendicant friars and their sale of indulgences, Wycliffe preached the gospel of Christ as opposed to the doctrines and traditions that, he charged, had built an edifice of "salvation" on useless works and foolish superstitions. Eventually he gave the British their greatest weapon against apostate Christianity: the first-ever English translation of Scripture. Now, more than ever, England—and other countries as well (as his work spread)—had a chance to learn truths of salvation as opposed to the doctrines and decretals of the ecclesiastical hierarchy. Though eventually summoned to appear at Rome (which would have meant the stake), Wycliffe died of natural causes.

Angry that their prey had escaped them, and revealing the spirit behind them, church leaders—more than 40 years after his death—exhumed Wycliffe's body, burned it, and threw his ashes in a brook, where they spread far and wide.

Little did they understand the symbolism of their deed.

Wycliffe wasn't the only Catholic to defy his church. In the fifteenth century John Huss of Bohemia (a region in the former Czechoslovakia) dared to proclaim the truth of God's Word. Although summoned to the Vatican, Huss remained in Prague under the protection of its king and queen. The pope had a trial anyway, condemned Huss, and placed the city of Prague under interdict, which supposedly meant that the gates of heaven would remain closed to the city's inhabitants until the pope opened them again. Because of the tumult the decree caused (an example of the theological ignorance of Europe under the medieval church), Huss left the city but didn't stop preaching.

Eventually hauled in chains before a vast council, Huss—already condemned—refused to recant. Immediately a ceremony of degradation began. After clothing him in a sacerdotal garment and vestments, the authorities again commanded him to recant.

"With what face, then, should I behold the heavens?" he replied. "How shall I look upon those multitudes of men to whom I have preached the pure gospel? No; I esteem their salvation more than this poor body, now appointed to death."[5]

The bishops removed the vestments he wore one by one, each bishop pronouncing a curse as he performed his part of the ceremony. Finally they put on his head a cone-shaped paper mitre painted with devils and the word "Archheretic."

The church turned Huss over to the secular authorities for execution. After fastening him to the stake, church leaders again, before a vast crowd, exhorted Huss to recant and save himself.

"What errors shall I renounce?" he answered. "I know myself guilty of none. I call God to witness that all I have written and preached has been with the view of rescuing souls from sin and perdition; and, therefore, most joyfully will confirm with my blood that truth which I have preached and written."[6]

As the flames engulfed him, Huss sang, "Jesus, Thou Son of David, have mercy on me!" with so loud and cheerful a voice that people heard him despite the crackling of flames until he could sing no longer and died.

But, as with Wycliffe, the church leadership's problems with those determined to follow the Bible didn't end with these deaths.

On the contrary, they had only just begun.

If Catholics such as Wycliffe and Huss were thorns in Rome's flesh, then the Augustinian monk Martin Luther was a dagger in the heart. Stubborn, unwavering, uncompromising, Luther had that fire in the belly needed to stare in the face of the most powerful and fearsome force in the West and not back down.

It is said that more has been written about Martin Luther than anyone in the history of Christianity except for Jesus Himself. And with good reason: his story is worth retelling.

As a young man, seeking peace with God and freedom from guilt, Luther entered a monastery. Haunted by doubts about his salvation, the young monk found help from the pious Catholic vicar John Staupitz, who turned Luther toward Christ and His salvation while also encouraging him to study and teach the Bible. Little did Staupitz, much less Luther, realize where it would lead.

The storm broke in the early 1500s when, needing funds for the building of St. Peter's Church in Rome, the pope started selling indulgences. Certain religious leaders told the masses that they could not only spare themselves punishment for their transgressions, but could also release their loved ones from purgatory—it would just cost them a little money, that's all. The moment their coins would clink against the bottom of the money chest, some assured them, the soul in whose behalf it had been paid would escape purgatory and go right to heaven.

The official appointed to conduct the fund-raising in Germany was a Dominican monk named Tetzel, who made the mistake of hawking his wares near Wittenberg, where Martin Luther taught. Having through his own study and experience arrived at a deeper understanding of salvation by faith alone, Luther protested the indulgences, stressing that salvation came not from paying money to some church official but only through the righteousness of Christ. Nothing but repentance toward God and faith in Christ can save the sinner, he said. "Indulgences," he wrote, "are most pernicious because they induce complacency and thereby impede salvation. Those persons are damned who think that letters of indulgence make them certain of salvation."[7] He attacked the concept that papal authority can release people from purgatory. "If the pope," he wrote, "does have the power to release anyone from purgatory, why in the name of love does he not abolish purgatory by letting everyone out?"[8]

Thus began the most important event in Christian history since the death and resurrection of Jesus Christ, an event still not over today, and, in fact, an event in danger of being overturned: the Protestant Reformation.

Thanks to Martin Luther, thoughtful Catholics all over Europe began losing confidence in many of the superstitions they had been raised on, and were instead seeking salvation through the merits of Jesus Christ alone. The masses, so long blinded by human rites and human mediators, now turned in faith and penitence toward Christ and His crucifixion as the only means of salvation.

Luther, though threatened, damned, and cursed, held his ground, challenging his opponents to show from the Bible his error. Eventually he appeared before an assembly of political and church leaders at the Diet of Worms in the early spring of 1521, one of the defining moments in Western history.

"The scene lends itself to dramatic portrayal. Here was Charles, heir of a long line of Catholic sovereigns—of Maximilian the romantic, of

Ferdinand the Catholic, of Isabella the Orthodox—scion of the house of Hapsburg, Lord of Austria, Burgundy, the Low Countries, Spain, and Naples, Holy Roman Emperor, ruling over a vaster domain than any save Charlemagne, symbol of medieval unities, incarnation of a glorious if vanishing heritage; and here before him a simple monk, a miner's son, with nothing to sustain him save his own faith in the Word of God." [9]

As he stood before the emperor, a church spokesman pointed Luther to a collection of his writings and asked two questions: Were they his? Would he retract them? To the first he answered yes, and to the second, he said that "seeing that it is a question which has reference to faith, and the salvation of souls—a question which concerns the Word of God, the greatest and most precious treasure either in heaven or earth—I would act rashly if I were to answer without reflection." He required time to think over his reply. [10] The authorities granted it.

The next day, in an even larger hall with more people, Luther—calm, peaceful, yet brave and noble—stood before some of the most powerful personages in Europe.

"Most Serene Emperor, you illustrious princes and gracious lords," he said, "I appear this day before you in all humility, according to your command, and I implore Your Majesty and Your August Highnesses, by the mercies of God, to listen with favor to the defense of a cause which I am well assured is just and right. I ask pardon, if by reason of my ignorance, I am wanting in manners that should befit a court; for I have not been brought up in king's palaces, but in the seclusion of a cloister." [11]

Then, in response to the request that he recant, he said that because even some of his enemies agreed with certain positions of his works, he saw no need to retract them. His were not the only writings to expose ecclesiastical corruptions. To retract them would only strengthen the tyranny of the church leadership in Rome and, he said, open the way for more impieties. Although he had attacked certain individuals (such as the pope) and though he admitted his tone wasn't always prudent, he still would not repudiate them, because to do so would embolden the enemies of truth.

"Therefore, Most Serene Emperor, and you illustrious princes, and all, whether high or low, who hear me, I implore you by the mercies of God to prove to me by the writings of the prophets and apostles that I am in error. As soon as I shall be convinced, I will instantly retract all my errors, and will myself be the first to seize my writings, and commit them to the flames." [12]

After he had defended himself even more (and then repeated the same words in Latin), the authorities again angrily demanded that he retract his charges.

His response has echoed down through history: "Since Your Most Serene Majesty and Your High Mightiness require of me a simple, clear, and direct answer, I will give one, and it is this: I cannot submit my faith either to the pope or to the councils, because it is as clear as noonday that they have often fallen into errors, and even into glaring inconsistency with themselves. If then I am not convinced by proof from the Holy Scripture or by cogent reasons; if I am not satisfied by the very texts that I have cited; and if my judgment is not in this way brought into subjection to God's Word, I neither can nor will retract anything: for it cannot be right for a Christian not to speak his conscience." Then studying the assembly before whom he stood, and which held in its hands his life or death, he said, "I stand here, and can say no more: *God help me,* amen." [13]

God did. In fact, whatever Luther's faults, prejudices, and mistakes, the Lord used him to start a movement whose impact was so great that the present world would be unrecognizable without it. Through Luther's fearless attempt to be faithful to God's Word, the light of Scripture exposed almost a thousand years of error and superstition. The power of God's Word pushed back layers of religious darkness. The Holy Spirit moved upon the minds of millions to seek salvation in Christ alone, without interference from an earthly power that had taken upon itself the prerogatives that belong only to the Lord. Luther won a mighty battle for the cause of truth. Thanks to this faithful but flawed warrior for God, the front lines in the great controversy between Christ and Satan had dramatically shifted, even if the battle remained far from over.

---

[1] Josephus, *The Works of Josephus: Antiquities of the Jews and a History of the Jewish Wars,* trans. William Whiston (Philadelphia: David McKay Publisher), Book V, Chapter XII, p. 826.

[2] Clyde Manschreck, *A History of Christianity: From Persecution to Uncertainty* (Chicago Theological Seminary, 1974), p. 28.

[3] Thomas Hobbes, *Leviathan,* in *Great Books of the Western World* (Chicago: Encyclopedia Britannica, 1971), p. 278.

[4] John Charles Ryle, "What We Owe to the Reformation," *Liberty*, November–December 1983, p. 12.

[5] John Foxe, *Foxe's Book of Martyrs* (New York: Holt, Reinhart, and Winston, 1965), p. 109.

[6] *Ibid.*

[7] Quoted in Roland H. Bainton, *Here I Stand* (New York: Mentor Books, 1978), pp. 62, 63.

[8] *Ibid.*, p. 62.

[9] *Ibid.*, p. 141.

[10] J. H. Merle D'Aubigne, *History of the Great Reformation of the Sixteenth Century in Germany and Switzerland* (New York: American Tract Society, 1846), vol. 2, book 7, p. 228.

[11] *Ibid.*, p. 233.

[12] *Ibid.*, p. 234.

[13] *Ibid.*, p. 236.

CHAPTER THREE

BLOOD AND LIGHT

I f Wycliffe and Huss had flickered in the night, Martin Luther burned across Europe in waves of light that devoured the darkness. The darkness resisted, of course, and the battle against the gospel was fierce, violent, always desperate, and at times uncannily subtle.

Satan soon found an even more effective means to hinder truth than bulls, anathemas, and the stake—and that was professed Reformers themselves. Many slipped into radical fanaticism and extremism, all of which threatened to undo the progress spiritual truth had made. Claiming divine revelation, some of the fanatics asserted that heaven had commissioned them to complete the Reformation feebly and deficiently (they claimed) started by Luther. In reality, they were following their own emotions, passions, and imaginations, sometimes unleashing spasms of lawlessness, violence, and debauchery. Having rejected the foundation upon which the Reformation rested (the Word of God as the all-sufficient rule of faith and practice), these men were doing exactly what Satan wanted.

Among the most dangerous was Jan Bockelson, who established a military Communistic regime in the city of Munster in Germany. Claiming divine revelation, Bockelson legalized polygamy (he took 15 wives) named himself King David, and heralded the Second Coming. After a terrible battle in which many inhabitants starved to death, Munster fell to an army that tortured Bockelson before hanging his mangled corpse in a cage.

Papal authorities blamed such fanaticism on Luther and his teachings. Luther, fighting Rome on one hand and the fanatics on the other, constantly wielded his great weapon against both: the Bible. Eventually he translated the New Testament into German. Fearful, Rome worked furiously to stop the Bible's from spreading, but the more it condemned and prohibited the Scriptures the more eager the people were to read them. Monks wandered through Germany selling the works of Martin Luther and his Bible translation. Catholics of all ranks—laborers, artisans, and nobility—studied Scripture, and as they did, the shackles of superstition and error began to shatter.

Persecution raged across northern Europe. John Foxe described what happened in Germany to Protestants:

"The generals Tilly and Pappenheim, having taken the Protestant city by storm, upwards of twenty thousand persons, without distinction of rank, sex, or age, were slain during the carnage, and six thousand were drowned in attempting to escape over the River Elbe. After this fury had subsided, the remaining inhabitants were stripped naked, severely scourged, had their ears cropped, and being yoked like oxen were turned adrift. . . . The cruelties used by the imperial troops, under Count Tilly in Saxony, are thus enumerated. Half strangling, and recovering the person again repeatedly. Rolling sharp wheels over the fingers and toes . . . tying cords round the head so tightly that the blood gushed out of the eyes, nose, ears, and mouth . . . putting powder in the mouth and setting fire to it, by which the head was shattered to pieces . . . hanging Protestants up by the legs, with their heads over a fire, by which they were smoke dried. . . . Hanging, stifling, roasting, stabbing, burning, broiling, crucifying, immuring, poisoning, cutting off tongues, noses, ears, etc., sawing off the limbs, hacking to pieces, and drawing by the heels through the streets." [1]

Despite the untold thousands and thousands (eventually millions) who sealed their testimony with blood, nothing could stop the spread of the recovered gospel. As in the early days, when pagan Rome persecuted the church, the same thing happened when centuries later papal Rome fought the Reformation: biblical truth spread even more rapidly. The violence simply made the contrast between darkness and light clearer, and the choice between truth and error that much starker.

The gains made by Protestants came, however, at great cost. They shed much blood, sweat, and tears. Good people on both sides, often innocent, suffered greatly.

Yet the reform faith continued to spread, even beyond Germany. Though not without personal flaws or theological errors, both John Calvin in Geneva and Ulrich Zwingli in Zurich bravely led the people to a greater understanding of the Bible.

In France, even before the appearance of Luther, spiritual lights began to glow. The aged Jacques Lefévre, a devout Roman Catholic, began to see the great truth of salvation by faith in Christ alone. One of his students, William Farel, zealous in the cause of the medieval church, soon became an equally ardent proponent for the New Testament teaching of Christ. The ancient understanding of the gospel penetrated even among nobles such as knight Louis de Berquin, soon scorned by his enemies as one worse than Martin Luther himself. Imprisoned three times as a heretic, each time a sympathetic king would release Berquin, and once more, using the Bible as his only defense, the knight would battle for the truth of God's Word.

In Paris, after Berquin challenged the monks to compare the teachings of the Bible with the traditions of the church, someone desecrated an image of the virgin Mary. Taking advantage of the situation, the monks had Berquin arrested, convicted, and sentenced to die. At noon, tied to the stake in the public square before a massive crowd, Berquin tried to address the people, but the monks, fearful of what he might say, began to shout, soldiers clashed their weapons, and the noise drowned out his voice.

The executers strangled Berquin, then burned his body.

Sometimes, unfortunately, the Protestants themselves were their own worst enemies. When some zealous but imprudent Protestants placed all over

France placards that attacked the Mass, the French church authorities used the act to begin a systematic assault against them. With the full sanction of the king (himself outraged when someone nailed one of the placards to the door of his own bedroom!), the authorities dragged Lutherans from their homes in Paris and burned them at the stake.

"The scaffolds were distributed all over the quarters of Paris, and the burnings followed on successive days, the design being to spread the terror of heresy by spreading the executions. The advantage, however, in the end, remained with the gospel. All Paris was enabled to see what kind of men the new opinions could produce. There was no pulpit like the martyr's pile. The serene joy that lit up the faces of the men as they passed along . . . to the place of execution, their heroism as they stood amid the bitter flames, their meek forgiveness of injuries, transformed, in instances not a few, anger into pity, and hate into love, and pleaded with resistless eloquence in behalf of the gospel."[2]

The New Testament understanding of the gospel made it to the Netherlands as well, but again not without opposition. To read the Bible, to hear or preach it, or even to speak about it, meant death. To pray to the Lord in secret in a Protestant manner, to refrain from bowing before an image, or to sing a psalm were capital crimes. The authorities still condemned those who recanted from their "errors." Men perished by the sword while women were buried alive.

One account tells of a whole family charged with staying away from Mass and worshiping at home.

When questioned, the youngest son answered: "We fall on our knees, and pray that God may enlighten our minds and pardon our sins; we pray for our sovereign, that his reign may be prosperous and his life happy; we pray for our magistrates, that God may preserve them."[3]

The punishment for their terrible crime?

The father and one son were burned at the stake.

In England, meanwhile, the work of William Tyndale, who wanted to produce a Bible translation better than Wycliffe's, had a great impact. Having had to flee the island because of ecclesiastical opposition, he continued his work on the continent, where he completed an English version of the New Testament that others smuggled into Britain. Arrested in Holland, he was imprisoned, tried, convicted, bound to a stake, strangled, and burned.

The English Reformers, often men of learning and stature, built the foundation of their movement upon the same one on which Wycliffe, Huss, Luther, and others built theirs: the infallible authority of the Holy Scriptures as the rule of faith and practice. They denied the right of ecclesiastical leaders, church councils, church tradition, and kings to control the conscience in religious matters. The Bible was their final authority, and by it alone would they test all doctrine. For their faith, for their devotion to the Word of God, many lost their lives.

Among those were Nicholas Ridley and Hugh Latimer, whose executions *Foxe's Book of Martyrs* has immortalized.

"The place of death was on the north side of the town, opposite Baliol College. Dr. Ridley was dressed in a black gown furred, and Mr. Latimer had a long shroud on, hanging down to his feet. . . . When they came to the stake, Dr. Ridley embraced Latimer fervently, and said to him: 'Be of good heart, brother, for God will either assuage the fury of the flame, or else strengthen us to abide it.' . . . The smith placed an iron chain about their waists, and Dr. Ridley bid him fast it securely; his brother having tied a bag of gunpowder about his neck, gave some also to Mr. Latimer. . . . A lighted fagot was now laid at Dr. Ridley's feet, which caused Mr. Latimer to say, 'Be of good cheer, Ridley, and play the man. We shall this day, by God's grace, light up such a candle in England as I trust will never be put out.'"[4]

It wasn't. In fact, the light spread so well that eventually Protestantism took hold as the established faith in England.

Unfortunately, though the Church of England denied the supremacy of the pope and rejected many of Rome's teachings, it still retained many ancient traditions. Worse, it quickly departed from the purity and simplicity of the gospel characteristic of the early years of the Reformation. Though Protestants only rarely employed the horrible cruelties used so readily by medieval Christianity, they did not understand the principles of religious liberty and denied the right of every person to worship according to the dictates of conscience.

All were, in fact, required to accept the doctrines and observe the forms of worship decreed by the official church. Dissenters suffered. The authorities, whether civil or ecclesiastical, expelled pastors from their pulpits for not following prescribed forms. People endured fines, even imprisonment, if they attended services not sanctioned by church officials.

Though free from Rome, Britain—under the rule of the Church of England—declined into its own era of great spiritual darkness. Her Protestant rulers proved no less faithful to the ancient New Testament gospel than the medieval church had. Natural religion, as opposed to clear and distinct Bible doctrines, began to infiltrate much British religious thought. Most important, too, the great truth of justification by faith alone, so clearly taught by Luther and discovered at such a great cost, had almost lost its influence.

England desperately needed another reformation. And, in His time and in His great providence, the Lord raised up just the man to bring it.

A loyal son of the Anglican Church as Luther had been of his, John Wesley (like Luther) had hungered for freedom from the tormenting guilt of sin. Because the seminal truth of Christianity—Christ crucified as humanity's only hope of salvation—had again faded (this time among Protestants), Wesley struggled in vain (like Luther) to free himself from the condemnation that sin brings. Then, through the influence of some German Christians who had convinced him that he must renounce all dependence upon his own works for salvation and lean only, and totally, upon "the Lamb of God, which taketh away the sins of the world," Wesley finally found the peace and assurance he had failed to obtain through years of rigorous self-denial, self-abnegation, and prayer.

Thus while still living a self-denying and prayerful existence—not as *the means* of salvation but *the fruit*—Wesley devoted his life to spreading the concept across the British Isles. Despite years of scorn, derision, and persecution, he ignited a great revival in his country as he preached justification through faith in the atoning blood of Jesus, and the renewing power of the Holy Spirit to conform lives to the will of God.

During the course of his long ministry, Wesley confronted numerous theological errors that had eroded the soul of the English church. One was the belief that God predestined some to be saved, others to be lost, and that individuals had no choice in the matter. Another error held that those predestined to to salvation can never lose their salvation and, even worse, whatever they did, no matter how evil, couldn't be sinful because they were God's elect.

Such false doctrines had close links to the erroneous belief that Christ's death on the cross meant that the moral law, the Ten Commandments, was no longer binding upon Christians, who were saved by faith, apart from the law (Romans 3:20). Wesley railed against such teachings, especially the one asserting that Calvary had nullified the Ten Commandments. Just because the law couldn't save people, Wesley realized, it didn't mean they were now free to sin. In fact, the Bible defines sin as violation of God's law. "Whosoever committeth sin transgresseth also the law: for sin is the transgression of the law" (1 John 3:4).

Wesley understood the inherent contradiction of

those who would preach against sin yet teach that God had done away with the law (a false doctrine still advocated today). As 1 John 3:4 says, sin is defined by law. Without law, sin couldn't exist. If sin is real, then the law must be too. How could the law be done away with, and sin still be a reality?

Wesley correctly affirmed the closest connection between the law and the gospel: the law pointed the sinner to his or her need of the gospel, while the gospel pointed the sinner to the law, which defined sin.

His teachings, firmly rooted in Scripture, profoundly transformed England. Some historians credit his influence with sparing England from its own version of the French Revolution. God alone knows how many lives his witness lifted from degradation and ruin. His life bears eloquent and powerful testimony to what God can do through someone who surrenders himself to the power of the Holy Spirit in an earnest desire to preach Christ's death on the cross and the salvation it accomplished for all those who would make it the overriding reality of their lives.

Though some nations in Europe gladly, if at great cost, welcomed the Reformation, others—after much conflict—rejected it, at even greater cost. France provides a striking example. From the cold-blooded murder of the Albigensians and the Huguenots, to the St. Bartholomew Massacre, in which an estimated 70,000 Protestants perished, Christ's followers suffered more in France than perhaps anywhere else in Europe.

It was in the French Revolution—where the

same spirit that fought the gospel through the church now worked through atheism and anticlericalism to bring about the same violent suppression of the truth of the Bible—that the French reaped the consequences of their rejection of the Protestant Reformation. Now, however, instead of justifying such violence in the name of God, Christ, and Christianity, the revolution's leaders did it in the name of reason, science, and antisuperstition. Just as Rome thought to suppress the Bible, the radicals of the French Revolution attempted the same. Either way, Satan exulted, for he knew that if read, accepted, and obeyed, the Bible would unmask his deceptions.

The French Revolution was the inevitable result of centuries of willful ignorance. Deprived of the elevating truths of the Bible, and thus shrouded in ignorance and superstition, the French lacked the moral and spiritual foundations they needed for the self-government they so fanatically foisted upon themselves. They had thrown away decency, self-restraint, and the law of God Himself.

On the spot where the medieval church had burned the first French martyrs of the Protestant faith, the first victims of the rule of reason now lost their heads on the guillotine. In rejecting the gospel, France opened the door to degradation and ruin. When French society cast aside the restraints of God's law, human law could no longer hold back the seething tides of human passion. The nation boiled in bloodshed and anarchy. Scenes of horror convulsed the cities. The persecution that some French priests had brought upon others now fell upon their own heads.

The dungeons were filled not with those seeking to live by the gospel, but with those who had once suppressed the gospel. No one—Christian, deist, atheist—was safe. One recent book on the French Revolution describes some of the violence:

"From early on in December the guillotine went into action at a much greater tempo. As in Paris, pride was taken in its mechanical efficiency. On the eleventh of Nivose, according to scrupulous accounts kept, thirty-two heads were severed in twenty-five minutes; a week later twelve heads in just five minutes.

"For the most eager terrorists, though, this was still a messy and inconvenient way of disposing of political garbage. Citizens in the streets around the Place des Terreaux, on the Rue Lafont, for example, were complaining about the blood overflowing the drainage ditch that led from beneath the scaffold. A number of the condemned, then, were executed in mass shootings on the Plaine des Brotteaux. . . . As many as sixty prisoners were tied in a line by ropes and shot at with cannon. Those who were not killed outright by the fire were finished off with sabers, bayonets, and rifles. On the fourth of December, Dorfeuille wrote to the president of the convention that a hundred and thirteen inhabitants of 'this new Sodom' had been executed on a single day. . . . Every atrocity the time could imagine was meted out to the defenseless population. Women were routinely raped, children killed, both mutilated. . . . General Crouzat's column forced two hundred old people, along with mothers and children, to kneel in front of a large pit they had dug; they were then shot so as to tumble in their own grave. Some who attempted to flee were struck down by the hammer of a local patriot mason. Thirty children and two women were buried alive when earth was shoveled onto the pit."[5]

However gruesome, however satanic, France's war on the Bible and the gospel—first through the clerics, then through the atheists—failed miserably. Voltaire's words, "I am weary of hearing people repeat that twelve men established the Christian religion. I will prove that one man may suffice to overthrow it" turned out to be the vain empty boast of an arrogant and deceived man. Even to this day, despite untold enemies who have attempted to suppress it by violence or nullify it by arguments and sophistry, the Bible still stands as the immovable revelation of God's love. It is the firm foundation upon which humanity can know the wonderful truths of salvation in Jesus Christ—truths that logic, reason, and natural science can never in and of themselves reveal.

[1] John Foxe, *Foxe's Book of Martyrs,* pp. 168, 169.

[2] J. A. Wylie, quoted in Ellen G. White, *The Great Controversy* (Mountain View, Calif.: Pacific Press Pub. Assn., 1911), p. 226.

[3] *Ibid.,* p. 240.

[4] Foxe, p. 237.

[5] Simon Schama, *Citizens* (New York: Random House, 1989), pp. 782, 783, 791.

CHAPTER FOUR

IN THE HOLY OF HOLIES

Despite the bloody break with Rome, the English Reformers retained enough medieval customs and ceremonies to drive many away not only from the *Church* of England, but from England itself. Persecuted for refusing to say certain prayers or for not believing specific doctrinal details, thousands fled to the New World.

Yet the persecuted eventually became persecutors themselves. Though not as violent as the medieval church, the Pilgrims were just as intolerant. It took centuries after the first English settlers arrived for the principles of religious liberty, as depicted in Scripture, to be established in the United States. Painfully aware of the blood and tears of religious intolerance that soaked the Old World, America's founders determined to avoid that problem in the new.

Understanding that humanity's relationship to God had to be voluntary, and that no external power should coerce religious belief and worship, America's founders boldly separated church and state. Because

43

government by its very nature must use force (the power of law), and because religion by its very nature mustn't be forced, the Constitution's framers sought to keep religion and government as far apart as possible. The result was, perhaps, the noblest aspect of the American experiment: religious freedom for all faiths.

As tidings spread of a land where people could worship according to their conscience, thousands risked everything to cross the Atlantic for America, where they were granted freedoms once only dreamed about. Protestants from all over Europe overwhelmed America's shores. The Bible was the foundation of their lives, faith, culture, and laws. Despite hardships, struggles, and severe challenges, a new world began, one in which church and state were separate, in which law-abiding people could believe and practice religion as they wished, and in which all faiths could thrive.

For various reasons, however, Protestantism soon fell into decline. These churches—as well as their Protestant brothers and sisters in Europe—while highly favored in receiving the great blessings of the Reformation, now failed to progress spiritually. Though individuals sporadically arose to proclaim new truth and refute old error, most American Protestants were content to believe as their predecessors had. Formalism, doctrinal error, and even superstitions began more firmly to entrench themselves. By the nineteenth century the Protestants needed reform as much as the Catholics had in the time of Luther.

Satan exulted. Unable any longer to halt the spread of the Bible, he worked with cunning diligence to nullify its impact. Though almost everyone owned a Bible, few really understood or even read it, let alone lived by its teachings. Instead of upholding and defending the faith once delivered to the saints, Protestants clung to what were now old traditions and dusty doctrines. Even more important, the principles that cost the early Reformers so much now began to weaken or vanish, even in free America, despite the fact that the nation allowed truth every opportunity to be proclaimed from rooftop, doorway, and pulpit, with nary an inquisitor to stand in the way.

Not all American Protestants slept, however. Many riveted their eyes and hearts to the Word of God, and one teaching that jumped from the pages and rattled their souls was that of the Second Coming. From the day when Adam and Eve turned their sorrowing step from Eden, the Promised One's children have all looked for the Lord to break the destroyer's power and restore them to the earthly Paradise forfeited in the Fall. Far from being a footnote to Protestantism, the Second Coming is the consummation of what Scripture, faith, and salvation are all about.

Nineteenth-century America witnessed sporadic religious revivals, often centered on the belief that Christ would soon return. Many regarded various events— from the terrible Lisbon earthquake to one of the most fantastic meteor showers in recorded history—as fulfillment of Christ's warning that before His return there would be earthquakes as well as "signs in the sun, and in the moon, and in the stars" (Luke 21:25).

Among them was an honest and upright farmer

named William Miller, who, after a bout with skepticism and deism, became a diligent Bible student, particularly of the prophecies of Daniel and Revelation. Because of his studies he not only rejected many prevalent errors of the time (such as the belief in a millennial reign of peace before the end of the world) but became convinced that Christ's literal second coming was near.

Miller based his understanding partially on a prophecy from the book of Daniel. In Daniel 8 the prophet receives a vision in which four elements appear in chronological order: a ram, a male or he-goat, a little horn, and the cleansing of the sanctuary (Daniel 8:1-14). The identification of the first three elements are unmistakable: they were great world empires extending from his time to the end of the world. The prophecy identifies the ram as "Media and Persia" (verse 20), the he-goat as "Grecia" (verse 21), and the little horn, though not specifically named, had to be another world power—greater than the two previous ones—that would appear after Greece, persecute God's people, and exist to the end of time (verses 23-25). Only one power fits, and that was Rome, both in its pagan and Christian stages (Bible prophecy generally views both pagan and Christian Rome as one power).[1] "The true fulfillment of the little horn of Daniel 8," wrote church historian C. Mervyn Maxwell, "can only be the Roman Empire and its successor, the Roman church."[2]

The vision of the chapter then ended with the words "Unto two thousand and three hundred days; then shall the sanctuary be cleansed."

Media–Persia
Greece
Rome (pagan and papal)[3]
Sanctuary cleansed

Though identification of the first three aspects of the prophecy is irrefutable, what did the "cleansing of the sanctuary" mean? Speaking of three great world empires extending up through the present (indeed, the Christian, or papal, aspect of Rome is still a major player in world events)—the chapter nevertheless *climaxes* with this cleansing of the sanctuary. If the first three elements in the series are of major significance, and the series, in fact, concludes with the fourth element, then whatever that fourth and climactic event is, it also must be of major consequence.

Miller adopted the position (commonly held at the time) that the earth itself was the sanctuary referred to here, and the cleansing represented its purification by fire at the second coming of Christ. Even more important, because this event would happen at the end of a specific time prophecy (the 2300 days of verse 14), Miller logically assumed that if he could establish the date of the end of the 2300 days, he'd have the time of Christ's return, the climactic event of all human history.

To understand the text "And he said unto me, Unto two thousand and three hundred days; then shall the sanctuary be cleansed," Miller began with a widely recognized principle of biblical interpretation:

in most time prophecies a day symbolizes a year.[4] Thus the 2300 days really meant 2300 years, the longest time prophecy in Scripture.

The simplest way, of course, to discover when the 2300 years ended was to determine when it began. Unfortunately, Daniel 8 didn't give the starting point. In fact, though the prophecy explained the three previous elements (ram, goat, and little horn), it did not clarify the vision of the 2300 days (literally, in verse 26, "the evening and the morning"). Daniel specifically said in the chapter's last verse that he didn't understand it. "And I Daniel fainted, and was sick certain days; afterward I rose up, and did the king's business; and I was astonished at the vision, but none understood it" (verse 27). What "none understood" was the 2300-year prophecy. The passage already explained everything else.

The solution appears in the next chapter, in which after Daniel's prayer (Daniel 9:1-19) the angel Gabriel—the same angel interpreter in the vision of Daniel 8 (verse 16)—appears to the prophet and says that he will give him "understanding" (Daniel 9:22). Gabriel then tells Daniel to "understand the matter, and consider the vision" (verse 23)—the vision of the 2300 days.[5]

The angel immediately presents Daniel with another time prophecy—one that does have a starting point: "Seventy weeks are determined [literally, "cut off"] upon thy people and upon the holy city. . . . Know therefore and understand, *that from the going forth of the commandment to restore and to build Jerusalem* unto the Messiah the Prince shall be seven weeks, and threescore and two weeks: the street shall be built again, and the wall, even in troublous times. And after threescore and two weeks shall Messiah be cut off, but not for himself. . . . And he shall confirm the covenant with many for one week: and in the midst of the week he shall cause the sacrifice and the oblation to cease" (verses 24-27).

Though much has been written about this prophecy, just a few points will be emphasized here.[6] First, this prophecy, unlike the 2300 years, does have a starting point: "from the going forth of the commandment to restore and to build Jerusalem." Second, the prophecy, like that of the 2300 years, demands the day-year principle.

Fortunately, biblical history and archaeology have clearly established the command to restore and rebuild Jerusalem (after the Babylonian destruction in 586 B.C.) and that date is 457 B.C.[7]

The prophecy thus says that from this command (457 B.C.) "unto the Messiah the Prince shall be seven weeks, and threescore and two weeks"—in other words, it would be seven weeks, 60 weeks, and two weeks, or 69 weeks, until "the Messiah the Prince," whom Christian scholars almost universally acknowledge as Jesus.

Because 69 weeks equals 483 days (69 x 7), and because a day equals a year, the time span covers at least 483 years. Thus, according to this amazing prophecy, the Messiah should appear 483 years after the command in 457 B.C. to rebuild Jerusalem—exactly what happened. Adding 483 years to 457 B.C. comes to A.D.

27[8]—the time when Jesus, "the Messiah the Prince," was baptized and began His ministry.

The prophecy goes into specific details for the last week, or seven years (the first part covered only 69 weeks, or 483 years)—which included when Christ would be crucified.[9] The 70-week prophecy, then, covered 490 years—from 457 B.C. to A.D. 34.

The crucial point for Miller, however, was that this 490-year prophecy, with a definite starting date, was "cut off" (Daniel 8:26) from the larger 2300-year prophecy, which didn't have a definite starting date. With the 457 B.C. established, Miller added 2300 years and came to 1844—the end point of the 2300-year prophecy, or when the "sanctuary" would be "cleansed." The following charts explain how the prophecy works:

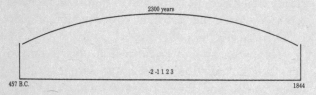

Either way, the numbers led to the same conclusions: 1844 was the end point of the 2300-year prophecy. Thus Miller—Bible in one hand, charts in

the other—began a great revival in churches throughout northeastern America, convinced that his Lord
was coming soon.

In 1844, to be exact.

C hrist, of course, didn't return in 1844.
Yet the dates were firm, as solid as numbers
themselves—and the entire prophecy was based on the
pivotal event of human history, Christ's first coming.

What, then, went wrong?

Certain (and rightly so) that the mistake *couldn't* be
in the dates and numbers, the early Adventists looked
to the *event* itself. Soon they discovered that Scripture
does not teach that the earth is the sanctuary. The
sanctuary, they began to understand, is in heaven, the
center of God's salvation activity for humanity, where
Christ intercedes in behalf of fallen men and women.
"Who is he that condemneth? It is Christ that died,
yea rather, that is risen again, who is even at the right
hand of God, who also maketh intercession for us"
(Romans 8:34).

And where does Christ, as our high priest, make
that intercession? The Bible is unequivocal: in the
heavenly sanctuary.[10]

"Now of the things which we have spoken this is
the sum: We have such an high priest, who is set on
the right hand of the throne of the Majesty in the
heavens; a minister of the sanctuary, and of the true
tabernacle, which the Lord pitched, and not man"
(Hebrews 8:1, 2). "But Christ being come an high
priest of good things to come, by a greater and more
perfect tabernacle, not made with hands, that is to say,

not of this building; neither by the blood of goats and calves, but by his own blood he entered in once into the holy place, having obtained eternal redemption for us" (Hebrews 9:11, 12).

These verses, in context, talk about the heavenly sanctuary, "the true tabernacle" made by God, not human beings. The book of Hebrews contrasts this "greater and more perfect tabernacle" (the heavenly sanctuary) to the earthly one of the Old Testament, in which the priests slew sacrificial animals and ministered their blood in the sanctuary—all symbolic of Christ's death and then ministry in the "true tabernacle." The earthly sanctuary was, in fact, modeled after the heavenly one, and its whole temple service reflected "the example and shadow of heavenly things, as Moses was admonished of God when he was about to make the tabernacle: for, See, saith he, that thou make all things according to the pattern shewed to thee in the mount" (Hebrew 8:5). That pattern revealed to him was that of the heavenly temple, seen also by John the revelator: "And the temple of God was opened in heaven, and there was seen in his temple the ark of his testament" (Revelation 11:19).

Scripture thus answers the question What is the sanctuary? It is the sanctuary in heaven, the model for the Hebrew sacrificial service in the Temple. More important, it is the place where Christ has gone, "a minister of the sanctuary, and of the true tabernacle, which the Lord pitched, and not man" (Hebrew 8:2).

However, the crucial question remained: What was *the cleansing* of this sanctuary that began in 1844?

For this question too the Millerites found their answer in the Word of God—the foundation of all revealed truth.

To begin with, they saw that the earthly sanctuary had two rooms for two distinct ministrations: the holy place, in which the priests served daily, and the Most Holy Place, which only the high priest entered, and then only on the Day of Atonement, which came once a year. They saw too that the earthly sanctuary itself went through a "cleansing" (Leviticus 16:16, 19)[11] on the Day of Atonement, when the high priest entered into the Second Apartment.

What fascinated the Millerites was Scripture's teaching of a purification, or cleansing, of the sanctuary in heaven—the sanctuary that served as the blueprint for the earthly. In the context of comparing the earthly sanctuary (which needed cleansing) to the heavenly, the book of Hebrews states: "It was therefore necessary that the patterns of things in the heavens should be purified with these; but the heavenly things themselves with better sacrifices than these. For Christ is not entered into the holy places made with hands, which are the figures of the true; but into heaven itself, now to appear in the presence of God for us" (Hebrews 9:23, 24).

In other words, just as the earthly sanctuary ("the patterns of the things in the heavens") had to be cleansed, or purified, how much more so would "heavenly things themselves" (the heavenly sanctuary) need cleansing. And this is what Christ, as the high priest, would do after He entered, not "the holy places made with hands" (the earthly sanctuary), but into the sanctuary in "heaven itself." And finally, because the book of Hebrews clearly taught that the earthly service, with its cleansing ritual, was merely "the example and shadow" of the heavenly sanctuary and service,[12] and because of the 2300-year prophecy placed the cleansing of the sanctuary many centuries after the last earthly sanctuary existed—Daniel 8:14 was unmistakably dealing with the cleansing of the heavenly sanctuary.

But what did that mean?

Just as in the earthly service the cleansing of the sanctuary was a solemn day of judgment, so the cleansing of the heavenly sanctuary, "the true tabernacle," is a day of judgment as well. In fact, because the earthly ritual merely symbolized the plan of salvation[13]—the day of judgment service, one part of the ritual, merely symbolized the real day of the judgment, the one the Scriptures constantly point to, the one expressed in Daniel 8:14 as the cleansing of the sanctuary.

Indeed, Daniel 7 and Daniel 8 are parallel prophecies, depicting through different symbols the rise and fall of great world empires and culminating in the end-time judgment that leads to the Second Coming. And the event in Daniel 7 that parallels the cleansing of the sanctuary in Daniel 8:14 is the great judgment scene that precedes the Second Advent.[14]

"The judgment shall sit, and they shall take away his dominion, to consume and to destroy it unto the end. And the kingdom and dominion, and the greatness of the kingdom under the whole heaven, shall be given to the people of the saints of the most High, whose kingdom is an everlasting kingdom, and all dominions shall serve and obey him" (Daniel 7:26, 27).

In other words, this judgment is another description of the cleansing of the heavenly sanctuary, the parallel event in the next chapter. No wonder Daniel gave the cleansing of the sanctuary so much prominence! It's the event that leads to Christ's return.

Christ Himself, in the parable of the wedding garment (Matthew 22), teaches a pre-Advent judgment. The king has a wedding for his son (verse 2), and many "both good and bad" (verse 10) come. When the king arrives, he sees a man not dressed in the wedding garment, a symbol of the perfect righteousness of Christ. Because he appears in judgment without the robe of Christ's righteousness, the guest is cast out, where there is "weeping and gnashing of teeth" (verse 13).

Talk about judgment! As Scripture says: "The Lord shall judge his people" (Hebrews 10:30), and Daniel 8:14 shows when this judgment actually began.

Thus letting the Bible interpret itself, and letting the Old Testament sanctuary service reveal great truths about Christ's death and high priestly ministry, many Millerites eventually understood their mistake. Rather than coming to the earth in 1844, Christ, our heavenly intercessor, entered the Second Apartment of the sanctuary in heaven, where He began the great work of judgment that would culminate in His return. Like the disciples, who misunderstood the nature of the Saviour's earthly ministry (and thus endured keen disappointment, at least at first, at His death), these Millerites, greatly heartened by this new light from the Scriptures, began a task that will not cease until

Jesus Christ, as He has promised again and again, comes in the clouds of glory.

<hr />

[1] For a detailed study on how this and other prophecies in Daniel as well as other books of the Bible were historically applied to Rome, both pagan and Christian, see LeRoy Edwin Froom, *The Prophetic Faith of Our Fathers* (Washington, D.C.: Review and Herald Pub. Assn., 1950).

[2] C. Mervyn Maxwell, *God Cares* (Mountain View, Calif.: Pacific Press Pub. Assn., 1981), vol. 1, p. 154.

[3] For a detailed and scholarly Bible study on the identity of the little horn of Daniel 8 as pagan and Christian, or papal, Rome, see Gerhard Hasel, "The 'Little Horn,' the Heavenly Sanctuary, and the Time of the End: A Study of Daniel 8:9-14," in Frank Holbrook, *Symposium on Daniel* (Washington, D.C.: Biblical Research Institute, 1986), pp. 378-425.

[4] For a powerful, complete, and scholarly study on the day-year principle, see William Shea, *Selected Studies on Prophetic Interpretation* (Washington, D.C.: Review and Herald Pub. Assn., 1982), pp. 56-93.

[5] In fact, though Daniel 8 and 9 use two different words for "vision," the word for "vision" dealing specifically with the 2300 years, *mareh,* is the same word employed in verse 22, when Gabriel told Daniel to "understand the matter, and consider the *mareh.*" For more information, see Clifford Goldstein, *1844 Made Simple* (Boise, Idaho: Pacific Press Pub. Assn., 1988), pp. 43-46. For a deep study of the relationship between Daniel 8 and Daniel 9, see William H. Shea, "The Relationship Between the Prophecies of Daniel 8 and Daniel 9," in Arnold Wallenkampf and W. Richard Lesher, eds., *The Sanctuary and the Atonement* (Washington, D.C.: Biblical Research Institute, 1981), pp. 228-250.

Fascinating, too, is that not just Christians, but even Orthodox Jews, have seen the clear link between the vision of the 2300 days of Daniel 8 and the 70-week prophecy of Daniel 9. Here is one Jewish commentary on the link. "This [Daniel 9:23] refers to Daniel's vision in chapter 8 in which the part which disturbed him so (verse 14) is characterized as a *mareh*" (Nosson Scherman and Meir Zlotowitz, eds., *Daniel,* Artscroll Torah Series [Brooklyn: Mesorah Publications, 1989], p. 258.

[6] For a detailed study on this prophecy, see "The Seventy

Weeks of Daniel 9: An Exegetical Study," in *The Sanctuary and the Atonement,* pp. 252-276. Also *God Cares,* pp. 189-257.

[7] For the certainty of the 457 B.C. date as the starting point of this prophecy, see Arthur J. Ferch, "Commencement Date for the Seventy-Week Prophecy," in Frank Holbrook, ed., *70 Weeks, Leviticus, Nature of Prophecy* (Washington, D.C.: Biblical Research Institute, 1986), pp. 64-74. See also S. H. Horn and L. H. Wood, *The Chronology of Ezra 7* (Washington, D.C.: Review and Herald Pub. Assn., 1953) and E. G. Kraeling, *The Brooklyn Museum Aramaic Papyri* (New Haven, Conn.: Yale University Press, 1953).

[8] To derive what date 483 years from 457 B.C. will give, one would subtract 457 from 483, which gives the number 26, or A.D. 26, rather than 27. Miller first made the mistake of forgetting that the calendar doesn't work like regular numbers. In other words, a regular number line would go -3, -2, -1, 0, 1, 2, 3. The calendar, on the other hand, doesn't go 2 B.C., 1 B.C., 0, A.D. 1, A.D. 2, etc. The zero on the number line doesn't exist on the calendar, which goes directly from 1 B.C. to A.D. 1, which explains the one-year discrepancy, and why the date is A.D. 27 rather than A.D. 26.

[9] "In the seventh chapter of Ezra the decree is found. Verses 12-26. In its completest form it was issued by Artaxerxes, king of Persia, 457 B.C. But in Ezra 6:14 the house of the Lord at Jerusalem is said to have been built 'according to the commandment ['decree,' margin] of Cyrus, and Darius, and Artaxerxes king of Persia.' These three kings, in originating, reaffirming, and completing the decree, brought it to the perfection required by the prophecy to mark the beginning of the 2300 years. Taking 457 B.C., the time when the decree was completed, as the date of the commandment, every specification of the prophecy concerning the seventy weeks was seen to have been fulfilled.

"'From the going forth of the commandment to restore and to build Jerusalem unto the Messiah the Prince shall be seven weeks, and threescore and two weeks'—namely, sixty-nine weeks, or 483 years. The decree of Artaxerxes went into effect in the autumn of 457 B.C. From this date, 483 years extend to the autumn of A.D. 27. . . . At that time this prophecy was fulfilled. The word 'Messiah' signifies 'the Anointed One.' In the autumn of A.D. 27 Christ was baptized by John and received the anointing of the Spirit. The apostle Peter testifies that 'God anointed Jesus of Nazareth with the Holy Ghost and with power.' Acts

10:38. And the Saviour Himself declared: 'The Spirit of the Lord is upon me, because he hath anointed me to preach the gospel to the poor.' Luke 4:18. After His baptism He went into Galilee, 'preaching the gospel of the kingdom of God, and saying, The time is fulfilled.' Mark 1:14, 15.

"'And he shall confirm the covenant with many for one week.' The 'week' here brought to view is the last one of the seventy; it is the last seven years of the period allotted especially to the Jews. During this time, extending from A.D. 27 to A.D. 34, Christ, at first in person and afterward by His disciples, extended the gospel invitation especially to the Jews. As the apostles went forth with the good tidings of the kingdom, the Saviour's direction was: 'Go not into the way of the Gentiles, and into any city of the Samaritans enter ye not: but go rather to the lost sheep of the house of Israel.' Matthew 10:5, 6.

"'In the midst of the week he shall cause the sacrifice and the oblation to cease.' In A.D. 31, three and a half years after His baptism, our Lord was crucified. With the great sacrifice offered upon Calvary, ended that system of offerings which for four thousand years had pointed forward to the Lamb of God. Type had met antitype, and all the sacrifices and oblations of the ceremonial system were there to cease" (Ellen G. White, *The Great Controversy,* pp. 326-328).

[10] For a more detailed study, see Frank Holbrook, ed., *Doctrine of the Sanctuary* (Silver Spring, Md.: Biblical Research Institute, 1989).

[11] "And he shall make an atonement for the holy place, because of the uncleanness of the children of Israel, and because of their transgressions in all their sins: and so shall he do for the tabernacle of the congregation" (Leviticus 16:16). An atonement was also to be made for the altar, to "cleanse it, and hallow it from the uncleanness of the children of Israel" (verse 19).

[12] "Important truths concerning the atonement are taught by the typical service. A substitute was accepted in the sinner's stead; but the sin was not canceled by the blood of the victim. A means was thus provided by which it was transferred to the sanctuary. By the offering of blood the sinner acknowledged the authority of the law, confessed his guilt in transgression, and expressed his desire for pardon through faith in a Redeemer to come; but he was not yet entirely released from the condemnation of the law. On the Day of Atonement the high priest, having taken an offering from

the congregation, went into the most holy place with the blood of this offering, and sprinkled it upon the mercy seat, directly over the law, to make satisfaction for its claims. Then, in his character of mediator, he took the sins upon himself and bore them from the sanctuary. Placing his hands upon the head of the scapegoat, he confessed over him all these sins, thus in figure transferring them from himself to the goat. The goat then bore them away, and they were regarded as forever separated from the people.

"Such was the service performed 'unto the example and shadow of heavenly things.' And what was done in type in the ministration of the earthly sanctuary is done in reality in the ministration of the heavenly sanctuary. After His ascension our Saviour began His work as our high priest. Says Paul: 'Christ is not entered into the holy places made with hands, which are the figures of the true; but into heaven itself, now to appear in the presence of God for us.' Hebrews 9:24.

"The ministration of the priest throughout the year in the first apartment of the sanctuary, 'within the veil' which formed the door and separated the holy place from the outer court, represents the work of ministration upon which Christ entered at His ascension. It was the work of the priest in the daily ministration to present before God the blood of the sin offering, also the incense which ascended with the prayers of Israel. So did Christ plead His blood before the Father in behalf of sinners, and present before Him also, with the precious fragrance of His own righteousness, the prayers of penitent believers. Such was the work of ministration in the first apartment of the sanctuary in heaven" (White, *The Great Controversy,* pp. 420, 421).

[13] In fact, the whole earthly service was just a picture of the entire plan of salvation, from Christ's death on the cross to the judgment. The earthly sanctuary could never, in and of itself, solve the problem of sin. It only pointed to Christ's death and ministry. "For the law having a shadow of good things to come, and not the very image of the things, can never with those sacrifices which they offered year by year continually make the comers thereunto perfect. For then would they not have ceased to be offered? because that the worshipers once purged should have had no more conscience of sins. But in those sacrifices there is a remembrance again made of sins every year. For it is not possible that the blood of bulls and of goats should take away sins" (Hebrews 10:1-4).

[14] Daniel 7 and Daniel 8 are, indeed, parallel prophecies, depicting many of the same events. The following chart quickly summarizes their parallel nature:

Daniel 7	Daniel 8
Babylon (lion)	———
Media–Persia (bear)	Media–Persia (ram)
Greece (leopard)	Greece (goat)
Rome, pagan and Christian, or papal (fourth beast)	Rome, pagan and Christian, or papal (little horn)
Judgment in heaven	Cleansing of the sanctuary

CHAPTER FIVE

AMERICA IN PROPHECY

The temple of God was opened in heaven, and there was seen in his temple the ark of his testament" (Revelation 11:19). The "ark of his testament" was the ornate box that sat in the Second Apartment of the earthly sanctuary[1] ("the example and shadow of the heavenly"). This New Testament reference to the heavenly sanctuary points specifically and irrefutably to the Second Apartment, where Christ now ministers His blood in behalf of "the saints of the most high" (Daniel 7:22). The "ark of his testament" also contained the Ten Commandments, God's eternal moral code (Exodus 25:21; Deuteronomy 10:3, 5).

Thus those who by faith had followed their great High Priest into the Most Holy Place understood not only the great pre-Advent judgment but also the relevance of God's law. As they studied Scripture—*in its entirety*—the eternally binding character of the Ten Commandments soon became apparent. And at the very heart of that law—like a hinge connecting the two tablets of stone—they saw the long-neglected Sabbath commandment:

"Remember the sabbath day, to keep it holy. Six days shalt thou labour, and do all thy work: but the seventh day is the sabbath of the Lord thy God: in it thou shalt not do any work, thou, nor thy son, nor thy daughter, thy manservant, nor thy maidservant, nor thy cattle, nor thy stranger that is within thy gates: for in six days the Lord made heaven and earth, the sea, and all that in them is, and rested the seventh day: wherefore the Lord blessed the sabbath day, and hallowed it" (Exodus 20:8-11).

If the Ten Commandments, they asked themselves, are still relevant, and included in—even at the heart of—those commandments is the Sabbath, why do Christians observe the first day of the week, Sunday, as opposed to "the seventh day," Saturday, specified in Scripture as the holy Sabbath? No New Testament evidence showed that God had either changed or abolished the fourth commandment. *Why would the Lord alter the one commandment in the entire law that specifically points to Him as the Creator?* It was clear: God's law (including the seventh-day Sabbath) was binding, a truth made especially apparent in the three angel's messages of Revelation 14:6-12.

The first angel's announcement that "the hour of his judgment is come" (Revelation 14:7) refers to the closing work of Christ's ministration in the heavenly sanctuary, the judgment that, according to Daniel 8:14, began at the close of the 2300 years (1844). The message also calls people to "fear God, and give glory to him." Then it says "worship him that made heaven, and earth, and the sea, and the fountains of waters" (verse 7)—language lifted from the Sabbath commandment itself, and thus an unmistakable reference to that commandment. Finally, in allusion to all the commandments, the message culminates with: "Here is the patience of the saints: here are they that keep *the commandments of God*, and the faith of Jesus" (Revelation 14:12).

In those verses (and others) early Adventist Bible students found more support for their position regarding the judgment, the law, and the seventh-day Sabbath. The Lord calls His faithful to worship and love the Creator, and obedience to His law is an inseparable part of that worship and love. "This is the love of God, that we keep his commandments: and his commandments are not grievous" (1 John 5:3). Among those commandments is the fourth, proclaiming the seventh-day Sabbath. It refers to Him who made "heavens, and earth" and "the sea" (Exodus 20:11; cf. Revelation 14:7).

Also the book of Revelation contrasts those who worship God, keep His commandments, and have the faith of Jesus with those whose false doctrines and practices elicit the most solemn warning in all Scripture: "The third angel followed them, saying with a loud voice, If any man worship the beast and his image, and receive his mark in his forehead, or in his hand, the same shall drink of the wine of the wrath of God, which is poured out without mixture into the cup of his indignation" (Revelation 14:9, 10).

After proclaiming the fearsome consequences for those who "worship the beast and his image," as opposed to those who "worship him that made heaven, and earth, and the sea, and the fountains of waters" and "keep the commandments of God," it wouldn't be fair for the Lord to leave humanity in the dark about the meaning of the passage.

Which, of course, is why He hasn't.

The line of prophecy in which these symbols (which includes the terrible warning about the worship of the beast) begins is Revelation 12, with the dragon that sought to kill Christ just after His birth. The dragon represents Satan himself,[2] manifested—at that specific time—through the pagan phase of Rome, which did try to slay the newborn Messiah (Matthew 2:1-18).

The next chapter, Revelation 13, describes another beast, "like unto a leopard" (verse 2), to whom the dragon (in the form of pagan Rome) gave "his power, and his seat, and great authority." Only one world system even possibly fits this description because only one world system closely linked to pagan Rome rose right after it: "Christian," or papal, Rome, which did receive its power and authority from its pagan predecessor, whom it replaced (in fact, the name *Pontifex Maximus,* one of the pope's titles, used to belong to the Caesars!). This identification of the beast as the medieval church was the almost unanimous view of Protestants up until the twentieth century.

Of this beast Scripture says: "There was given unto him a mouth speaking great things and blasphemies. . . . And he opened his mouth in blasphemy against God, to blaspheme his name, and his tabernacle, and them that dwell in heaven. And it was given unto him to make war with the saints, and to over-come them: and power was given him over all kin-dreds, and tongues, and nations" (Revelation 13:5-7). This prophecy, nearly identical with the descriptions of the little horn in Daniel 7,[3] refers to the Roman church, particularly during the Dark Ages.

Another identification mark is that "power was given unto him to continue forty and two months" (verse 5), a time span depicted in Scripture as "a time, times, and half a time" (Revelation 12:14; Daniel 7:25) or "a thousand two hundred and threescore days" (Revelation 11:3). Time, times, and dividing of time ("time" is universally understood as "year") is three and a half years, or 42 months, or 1260 days (by prophetic reckoning). Application of the day-year principle proves that Christian, or papal, Rome, or at least this phase of it, would be a major power for more than a millennium (1,260 years, to be exact)—an amazingly accurate prediction given that Christian Rome, unlike any other institution in the West, has indeed been around that long!

Prophecy says about this beast power: "I saw one of his heads as it were wounded to death; and his deadly wound was healed: and all the world wondered after the beast" (Revelation 13:3). Thus Christian Rome would reign for more than a millennium (1,260 years) before it would receive a "wound" (obviously to its power) that would eventually heal. Papal Rome assumed political hegemony in the early sixth century, which puts the end of the 1,260 years in the late eigh-teenth or early nineteenth century. Here is still another incredible prophecy, especially considering that in the late eighteenth/early nineteenth century—about 200 years ago—the papacy did lose much of the political power it had long wielded. The dust jacket of a 1990 book by Catholic apologist Malachi Martin stated that it was "John Paul's purpose to free the papacy from the straightjacket of inactivity imposed upon it by the major secular powers *for 200 years.*"[4] Two hundred years ago is the late eighteenth/early nineteenth century, when—according to the 1,260-year prophecy—papal Rome's political dominance would end, at least temporarily. (Some exegetes, in fact, believe that the exact dates for the beginning and end of the 1,260 years can be proved!)[5]

Yet the prophecy doesn't end here. Another power appears, one that, according to the text, will have a preeminent role in the final events that usher in the second coming of Jesus.

At the end of the prophetic sequence dealing with the 1,260-year phase of Rome, a new world power appears: "I beheld another beast coming up out of the earth; and he had two horns like a lamb" (Revelation 13:11). In two distinct ways this beast differs from those before it. First, unlike most of the other great world powers depicted in Daniel 7 and alluded to in Revelation 12 (all portrayed as violent beasts of prey), this one appears lamblike, gentle. Second, the prophecy describes the beasts (or empires) in Daniel 7 as rising from turbulent water, symbols of massive populations and conquest and war.[6] In contrast, the lamblike beast rises from the earth, the distinction being that while the other great powers appeared amid the often densely populated nations of the old world, this one would arise from another background, one not heavily populated. Nor did it arise amid the overt strife so indicative of the preceding empires.

What world power arising around the late eighteenth or early nineteenth century (the end of the 1,260-year period) matches the symbols depicted in Revelation 12? Only one nation fits: the United States of America—a massive power that gained prominence in a manner relatively peacefully contrasted to the violent struggles of the previous powers. In fact, many commentators of the last century used almost the same language in describing the rise of the United States to great potential and prominence.[7]

Scripture then gives more details about it: "He had two horns like a lamb." Again, in contrast to the violent symbols of the other nations, Scripture depicts this power as having horns "like a lamb," an indication of gentleness, of goodness, of benevolence. In fact, the Bible employs a lamb to symbolize Jesus Christ,[8] indicative of the character that the new great power would manifest. And though the United States has had a sometimes checkered history, the *relative* benevolence of its laws, the unheard-of freedom it has established, the religious liberty it has enshrined, the wonderful refuge it has provided for the downtrodden of the world, make the lamb a perfect symbol, especially in the immediate context of the book of Revelation, which deals mostly with religious and spiritual elements (as opposed to political ones).

Unfortunately, the gentle qualities do not last.

Indeed, the lamblike beast will, the prophecy says, speak "as a dragon," and just as a lamb was a symbol of Christ, the dragon is a symbol of Satan. Obviously, the benevolent character of the United States (at least in the context of the spiritual issues of the book of Revelation) will radically change.

What does this transformation mean? What, according to the Bible, will be the role of the United States, now universally recognized as the "world's only superpower," in the final events of world history? What happens when the lamblike beast begins to speak as a dragon?

Given the solemnity of issues depicted in the book of Revelation, these are crucial questions—which, of course, is why the Lord has given us the crucial answers.

The prophecy depicting the United States says that, though first appearing like a lamb, this power will speak "as a dragon" and also will exercise "all the power of the first beast before him, and causeth the earth and them which dwell therein to worship the first beast, whose deadly wound was healed. . . . Saying to them that dwell on the earth, that they should make an image to the beast" (Revelation 13:11-14).

The prediction that the United States, speaking "as a dragon," will exercise "all the power of the first beast," warns of a time when the nation will become a religious persecutor. The "first beast," the one whose "deadly wound was healed," the one that the United States will emulate, is the medieval church.

Revelation, then, predicts that the United States, by exercising all the power of "the first beast," will display the same intolerance and persecution so clearly manifested in medieval Rome and the pagan nations that preceded it.

According to prophecy, the United States will cause "the earth and them which dwell therein *to worship the first beast, whose deadly wound was healed.* . . . Saying to them that dwell on the earth, that they should make *an image to the beast."*

These verses point to the *religious* character of the persecution, so unlike the United States now (in its lamblike phase). Considering the religious character of the medieval church ("the first beast"), and the fact that the United States will force "worship" of this beast (as opposed to those who "worship him that made heaven, and earth, and the sea, and the fountains of waters" [Revelation 14:7])—this nation, in direct opposition to the great principles of separation of church and state, will command some sort of religious form of worship that, in one manner or another, will pay homage to medieval Christianity.

How could "Protestant" America ever manifest the attributes of the beast? More than a century ago one writer answered the question with a prophetic accuracy that depicts the religiopolitical situation in America today: "When the early church became corrupted by departing from the simplicity of the gospel and accepting heathen rites and customs, she lost the Spirit and power of God; and in order to control the consciences of the people she sought the support of the secular power. The result was the papacy, a church that controlled the power of the state and employed it to further her own ends, especially for the punishment of 'heresy.' In order for the United States to form an image of the beast, the religious power must so control the civil government that the authority of the state will also be employed by the church to accomplish her own ends."[9]

Christian history constantly teaches one simple lesson: whenever the church has obtained secular power, it has employed it to punish dissent. Also, it's always an apostate church, one devoid of the Spirit, that seeks secular power to do what it can't accomplish through its spiritual authority because of its own lack of truth, holiness, and spiritual power.

According to prophecy, something similar will happen in the United States: an apostate church or group of churches will seize the reins of power and persecute those who refuse to worship "the image of the beast" (Revelation 13:15).[10] If the first beast was medieval Rome, which used the state to persecute religious dissent, then the "image of the beast," which the United States enforces, means that somehow popular Christianity in the United States will employ civil power to do the same!

Enter the Christian Right.

For more than 100 years many Bible students have predicted that Protestants in the United States would, by uniting in some way with each other—and with Roman Catholics—amass enough political power to persecute those who will refuse to worship the beast and his image.

Though prophecy doesn't reveal exactly how such events will unfold, the ascendancy of the Christian Right—with its bold and unabashed attempt to "reclaim America for Jesus Christ" (along with its attempts at unity with Roman Catholicism for political reasons)—appears to be the logical candidate to fulfill the biblical prediction.

The Christian Right consists of various strains of conservative Protestants who—though possessing conflicting theologies—have united for a single purpose: to amass political power in America and to make it in its own image.[11] In fact, back in 1984 one columnist unknowingly used language and concepts directly from Revelation regarding the role of the Christian Right: "It may be Ronald Reagan's most profound achievement as a politician, though it is hardly noticed in the established world. He has given political legitimacy, and power, to religious fundamentalists who want to make America into their own *image* as a 'Christian nation'" (italics supplied).

The Christian Right has attracted attention now, to say the least. Friends and foes alike acknowledge it as the most powerful grassroots political movement in America. The cover of *Time* (May 15, 1995) said it best: "Meet Ralph Reed, 33. His Christian Coalition is on a crusade to take over U.S. politics—and it's working."

Wrote one commentator in *The New Yorker:* "For the religious right, invisibility is no longer possible. From South Carolina to Oregon, state parties are falling under its sway. . . . Across the nation, the flag and the cross are becoming one."[12]

Whatever good the Christian Right seeks, which

is a lot (the first beast power, medieval papal Rome, instituted much good too), it also advocates some very troubling positions, one of the worst (especially from a prophetic perspective) being its subversion of separation of church and state, the very principle that not only has made America "lamblike" in the first place but which, as long as it remains implemented, would never allow the United States to "speak as a dragon."

Could the Christian Right—with its blatant attempt at political control and unabashed antipathy toward church-state separation (literally the foundation of our religious freedom)—be the power that makes America enforce "the image of the beast"? Only our Lord knows. For now, however, the movement— with its drive to impose a "Christian order" through the power of law—seems to be heading on a path to fulfill these words written more than a century ago: "When the leading churches of the United States, uniting upon such points of doctrine as are held by them in common, shall influence the state to enforce their decrees and to sustain their institutions, then Protestant America will have formed an image of the Roman hierarchy, and the infliction of civil penalties upon dissenters will inevitably result."[13]

Prophecy has revealed who the first beast is, and also what power will enforce the image of this beast upon the world. The question remains: How will such an image manifest itself, and how will it be imposed?

So far, from Scripture, a few points are clear: "the first beast" (Revelation 13:1-10, 12) is papal Rome in its early and medieval phase. The second beast, the lamblike one that will speak as a dragon, is the United States. According to prophecy, the United States will force the world to "worship the image of the beast," some act in homage to the first beast, medieval Christianity, "whose deadly wound has healed" (verse 12).

Revelation 14 teaches also that the issue in the last days will center on worship, involving those who "worship the beast and his image" (verse 9), as opposed to those who "worship him that made heaven, and earth, and the sea, and the fountains of waters" (verse 7) and who also "keep the commandments of God" (verse 12). Because Scripture depicts those who worship the Creator (in opposition to those who worship the beast) as people obeying the commandments of God, the issue regarding the worship of the beast must involve these commandments, particularly as they deal with worship. Those worshiping the Creator keep the Ten Commandments while those worshiping the beast and his image, apparently, don't.

By specifically calling people to worship the Creator, and even using language directly from the Sabbath commandment—the only commandment that, by pointing to the Lord as the Creator, bears witness to His claim upon human homage and worship (after all, people worship God because He is the Creator!)—Revelation 14 offers powerful evidence that the Sabbath commandment will be a crucial factor. Indeed, considering that the final conflict deals with an act of homage to the religiopolitical entity such as the papacy, and that the papacy did, in fact, institutionalize the shift of the Sabbath from the biblical seventh day to the nonbiblical first, the relevance of the Sabbath becomes obvious. Even more so, Scripture teaches that one characteristic of the first beast (as depicted in Daniel 7) is that it would "think to change times and laws" (Daniel 7:25). The early Roman church did make Sunday (as opposed to Sabbath) its "official" day of rest, thus attempting to alter divine law, particularly the only part that deals with time![14]

What's even more astonishing is that Roman Catholic sources have historically acknowledged the church's role in their attempt to transfer the Sabbath from the seventh day to the first:

"The Catholic Church for over one thousand years before the existence of a Protestant, by virtue of her divine mission, changed the day from Saturday to Sunday. We say by virtue of her divine mission, because He who called Himself the 'Lord of the Sabbath' endowed her with His own power to teach, 'he that heareth you, heareth Me'; commanded all who believe in Him to hear her, under penalty of being placed with the 'heathen and publican'; and promised to be with her to the end of the world. She holds her charter as teacher from Him—a charter as infallible as perpetual. The Protestant world at its birth found the Christian Sabbath too strongly entrenched to run counter to its existence; it was therefore placed under the necessity of acquiescing in the arrangement, thus implying the church's right to change the day, for over three hundred years. The Christian Sabbath is therefore *to this day* the acknowledged offspring of the Catholic Church as spouse of the Holy Ghost, without a word of remonstrance from the Protestant world."[15]

Consider also the following examples:

"*Question*—Have you any other way of proving that the church has power to institute festivals or precepts?

"*Answer*—Had she not such power, she could not have done that in which all modern religionists agree with her—she could not have substituted the observance of Sunday the first day of the week, for the observance of Saturday the seventh day, a change for which there is no Scriptural authority."[16]

"*Question*—By whom was it [the Sabbath] changed?

"*Answer*—By the governors of the church, the apostles, who also kept it; for St. John was in the Spirit on the Lord's day (which was Sunday). Apoc. 1:10.

"*Question*—How prove you that the church hath power to command feasts and holy days?

"*Answer*—By the very act of changing the Sabbath into Sunday, which Protestants allow of; and therefore they fondly contradict themselves, by keeping Sunday strictly, and breaking most other feasts commanded by the same church.

"*Question*—How prove you that?

"*Answer*—Because by keeping Sunday, they acknowledge the church's power to ordain feasts, and to command them under sin; and by not keeping the rest [of the feasts] by her commanded, they again deny, in fact, the same power."[17]

Some Protestants find themselves forced to admit that no scriptural evidence exists for Sunday worship. One leading Protestant exponent of Sunday has written: "We must admit that we can point to no direct command that we cease observing the seventh day and begin using the first day."[18]

How ironic that Protestants, so often adamant about using the Bible alone as the standard of faith, have instead—in something so fundamental as the one commandment that points to the Lord alone as worthy of worship—followed the dictates of the medieval church, which by "changing" one of God's commandments, has taken the prerogatives of God Himself.[19] One Catholic source expressed it perfectly: "The observance of Sunday by the Protestants is homage they pay, in spite of themselves, to the authority of the [Catholic] Church."[20]

Thus when Protestants in America use the power of the state to enforce Sundaykeeping, they will, by emulating the methods of the first beast, form an "image" to that beast. And all who conform—in direct opposition to the command that points to the Lord as Creator!—will indeed be worshiping the beast "whose deadly wound was healed" (Revelation 13:12).

Of course, many sincere, faithful Catholics and Protestants have kept, or even now keep, Sunday. None have worshiped, or even now worship, the beast or his image. However, when a religiopolitical coalition enforces the observance of the false Sabbath during a time when the world has been enlightened concerning the true sign of God's creative power and authority—only then will all who openly transgress a commandment of God for a commandment of the beast, in fact, be worshiping the beast.

But does the specific day really matter?

It does—not because of the day itself (as opposed to any other day), but because of *what it represents*. The *seventh-day* Sabbath points humanity back to the foundation of all reality—that God is the Creator of heaven and earth. Nothing Christians believe makes any sense apart from this fundamental fact. Therefore, to tamper with the outward symbol of God's creatorship—something so crucial that the Lord used an in-your-face symbol (unlike any other in Scripture) that reoccurs week after week without respite to remind us of it—is to undermine the essence of God's authority. The "change" of the Sabbath is the ultimate attempt at usurping the Lord's prerogatives. The Sabbath isn't about a day; it's about worshiping the Creator as He, in His sovereignty and authority, commands us to.

Though some have questioned whether a Sabbath/Sunday controversy could ever be an issue again in the secular West, that doubt was trounced in the summer of 1998 when Pope John Paul II issued a lengthy apostolic letter, *Dies Domini,* in which he urged people not only to start keeping Sunday holy, but to pass laws that will enforce it.

Without question, the Sabbath/Sunday issue is hot. And according to prophecy, it will blaze into prominence before Christ returns. In fact, the three angels' messages of Revelation 14—which emphasize crucial truths such as the "everlasting gospel" (verse 6), "the hour of his judgment" (verse 7), and the call to "worship" the Creator (verse 7)—also give the most fearsome warning ever issued in Scripture. The passage specifically speaks to those who worship the beast and his image: "The same shall drink of the wine of the wrath of God, which is poured out without mixture into the cup of his indignation" (verse 10).

Scripture is clear that all Christendom will divide into two classes—those who obey God's commandments and have the faith of Jesus, and those who worship the beast and his image and receive his mark (verses 9, 11).

And though the United States will renounce the very principles of freedom it once so valiantly heralded, though church and state will unite to trample on religious liberty, and though Protestants and Catholics will join politically to compel adherence to the false Sabbath, God will have a faithful people who will—despite the threat of economic sanctions and even death (Revelation 13:15-17)—refuse to compromise. And that's because their love of Jesus will not allow them to. "For this is the love of God, that we keep his commandments: and his commandments are not grievous" (1 John 5:3).

Even from the earliest days of the church, truth has never been popular. It is the same today. Many who profess love for God and respect for His law balk at the seventh-day Sabbath. Yet even the Old Testament, prior to the Christian era (when the change supposedly took place), taught that the seventh-day Sabbath was for all who loved and served the Lord.21 Many argue that Sunday has a long, firmly established tradition, and that great church figures have observed Sunday, which is all true. Yet the seventh-day Sabbath, the day Jesus Himself observed, is still the biblical Sabbath, and nothing in Scripture points to its being superseded or replaced with Sunday.

The Sabbath, in fact, *could not* have been transferred, because that would have meant a change in God's law, inconceivable in light of the cross. If anything could have abolished the law or even altered it, then Christ would not have had to die. He could have instead merely changed His law to meet humanity in its sinful fallen condition. After all, wouldn't altering or abolishing the law (which points out sin) have been a better option than the Son of God facing the penalty for humanity's transgression of that law? Of course. Yet it wasn't an option, which is why it didn't happen. Far, then, from abolishing the law, the cross of Christ proves its immutability.

The law, however, only reveals to humanity its sin. It provides no remedy. The gospel alone can free humanity from the condemnation that sin brings. Only by faith in the merits of a crucified and risen Saviour can humanity find pardon and peace. And only through repentance toward God, whose law human beings have transgressed, and through faith in Christ, who by His atoning sacrifice paid the complete penalty for all the world's sin, can sinful humanity be assured of eternal life. The great news about the good news is that our acceptance with God rests on what Christ has done for us, not upon what we can do ourselves. The law has nothing to do with saving us. On the contrary, the law is what condemns. Obedience and holiness are the results of salvation, not its means.

Of course, besides forgiving sin, the Lord works to transform hearts and give those saved by His blood a new life, one in which people walk "not after the flesh, but after the Spirit" (Romans 8:4). Though never meant to be salvific, the law was always a guide for those who follow Christ. "Do we then make void the law through faith? God forbid: yea, we establish the law" (Romans 3:31).

By the Word and by the Spirit God has revealed to all humanity the great principles of righteousness embodied in God's law. Those whom His blood has justified will seek to live in obedience to that law in word, thought, and deed. They will rely wholly upon His merits alone for their salvation—they are indeed in harmony with the will and commands of their Creator.

Yet much professed Christianity today denies this crucial truth. "Only believe," some declare—that's all that the Christian life is about. There's no need for striving, for self-denial, for putting away the perversions of the world. God's law, they declare, has been abolished (akin to saying that sin has been abolished as well, and as obviously false).

But what does the Word of God clearly state? "He that saith, I know him, and keepeth not his commandments, is a liar, and the truth is not in him. But whoso keepeth his word, in him verily is the love of God perfected: hereby know we that we are in him" (1 John 2:4, 5).

Time and again the Word of God promises victory, holiness, and sanctification to those who seek to obey the Lord in faith and humility. Though no Christian could ever claim sinlessness, through Jesus they have received the promise that they will have all the power of heaven in their striving against sin, against the drives of the flesh, against the temptations of the evil one. Satan knows that only by luring Christians into sin and leaving them there can he finally separate them from Christ.

"For whosoever is born of God overcometh the world: and this is the victory that overcometh the world, even our faith" (1 John 5:4). And even when a Christian falls and breaks God's law, the wonderful life-changing truth of the gospel is that he or she may go to Jesus, their risen Saviour, and with repentance and faith claim His merits, thus standing before the law once more without shame and remorse. "There is therefore now no condemnation to them which are in Christ Jesus, who walk not after the flesh, but after the Spirit" (Romans 8:1)—not now, and not (especially) in the great pre-Advent judgment in heaven.

I beheld till the thrones were cast down, and the Ancient of days did sit, whose garment was white as snow, and the hair of his head like the pure wool: his throne was like the fiery flame, and his wheels as burning fire. A fiery stream issued and came forth from before him: the judgment was set, and the books were opened" (Daniel 7:9, 10).

Daniel here depicts the great pre-Advent judgment, a reality he also expressed when he said: "I saw in the night visions, and, behold, one like the Son of man came with the clouds of heaven, and came to the Ancient of days, and they brought him near before him. And there was given him dominion, and glory, and a kingdom, that all people, nations, and languages, should serve him: his dominion is an everlasting dominion, which shall not pass away, and his kingdom that which shall not be destroyed" (verses 13, 14).

Here we see Christ ("the Son of man") not returning to the earth but rather, attended by the heavenly angels, going to the Father ("the Ancient of Days"); we see Christ in the Most Holy Place of the heavenly sanctuary, where He began the final plans of His heavenly ministry, the judgment (which began in 1844) that ultimately leads to the Second Coming.

"Judgment must begin at the house of God: and if it first begin at us, what shall the end be of them that obey not the gospel of God?" (1 Peter 4:17). "And again, The Lord shall judge his people" (Hebrews 10:30).

This pre-Advent judgment is, specifically, the examination of those who have professed Christ, all who have their names "written in heaven" (Luke 10:20). Having one's name in heaven doesn't automatically mean Christ in the heart. On the contrary, many professed Christians have revealed, by their deeds, that they served another power. Such individuals have been—and will continue to be—some of Satan's most effective agents. The great pre-Advent judgment will finally and forever separate the wheat and the tares among the church.

Meanwhile, all who have truly repented, who have truly surrendered their lives to Christ in faith and obedience, have nothing to fear in the judgment. The judgment is, in fact, good news, because God's people all have a substitute standing in their stead. Jesus Himself, who presents His own perfect life in place of the sinner's imperfect one. No matter how holy, obedient, and law-abiding such a person may be, even then none of them has the righteousness needed to get through the judgment. That is why Jesus, the divine intercessor, pleads His merits in their behalf. The pre-Advent judgment is the final, climactic application in behalf of the believer of what Christ accomplished at the cross.

Even as Satan, humanity's accuser, points out the faults and sins of Christ's followers, Jesus, their advocate, defends them, not by excusing their sins and shortcomings, but instead by showing their penitence and faith. The Saviour lifts His scarred hands before the Father and the holy angels and says: *"I know them by name; I have graven them on the palms of my hands."* Here is the only way any sinner can stand in judgment before God. It is why Christ intercedes in humanity's behalf in the heavenly sanctuary, where He "ever liveth to make intercession for" His followers (Hebrews 7:25). His intercession is as essential to the plan of salvation as was His death.

Thus while Christ, our high priest, still intercedes in our behalf, how important that all those who profess to follow Christ truly surrender themselves to Him in faith, repentance, and obedience. Though obedience can't save, it is the outward manifestation of faith in Christ. The working out of faith is the means by which human beings strengthen, affirm, and make perfect their faith. "Seest thou how faith wrought with his works, and by works was faith made perfect?" (James 2:22).

Solemn are the scenes connected with Christ's closing ministry in the sanctuary above. When His work ends, it will have finally and irrevocably decided, either for eternal life or eternal death, the case of every individual. Then all heaven will hear the proclamation: "He that is unjust, let him be unjust still: and he which is filthy, let him be filthy still: and he that is righteous, let him be righteous still: and he that is holy, let him be holy still. And, behold, I come quickly; and my reward is with me, to give every man according as his work shall be" (Revelation 22:11, 12).

---

[1] See Exodus 25 and 26.

[2] "The great dragon was cast out, that old serpent, called the Devil, and Satan, which deceiveth the whole world: he was cast out into the earth, and his angels were cast out with him" (Revelation 12:9).

[3] Daniel 7, one of the most important prophetic chapters in Scripture, irrefutably points to the medieval church. As we saw previously, Daniel sees a vision of four great beasts that rise out of the sea: a lion (verse 4), a bear (verse 5), a leopard (verse 6), and a terrible fourth beast with 10 horns (verse 7), out from which a terrible persecuting little horn power arises from among the horns of the fourth beast (verse 8). Commentators from the Reformation on (and even some Jewish scholars prior to the Reformation) identified these powers as: lion (Babylon); bear (Media-Persia); leopard (Greece); fourth beast (pagan Rome); little horn (Christian, or papal, Rome).

The identification of that little horn as the medieval church rests on numerous identifying marks. First, unlike the other powers, which are separate beasts, the little-horn power that comes out of pagan Rome isn't a separate beast. It's distinctly part of the fourth beast, which was pagan Rome, only now in a different, latter stage, the Christian, or papal, one. Also, among other things, the little horn is a blasphemous power (verses 7, 25). Persecuting God's people (verse 21), it would attempt to change "times and laws" (verse 25). For a detailed study of this prophecy, see William H. Shea, "Unity of Daniel," in Frank Holbrook, ed., *Symposium on Daniel* (Washington, D.C.: Biblical Research Institute, 1986), pp. 165-219.

It's important, too, to realize that the beast in Revelation 13 also has the attributes, not just of a leopard, but of a bear and a lion (Revelation 13:2)—another link to Daniel 7, as these are the symbols used for all the beasts before it.

[4] Malachi Martin, *The Keys of This Blood* (New York: Simon and Schuster, 1990). (Italics supplied.)

[5] Some Bible expositors, with good reason, give exact dates for this 1260-year period. According to them, it began in A.D. 538 when the papacy threw out the last of the barbarian tribes from Rome, and then ended exactly 1,260 years later, in 1798, when a French general took the current pope captive. One church historian, C. Mervyn Maxwell, writing about the specific incident when French General Berthier took the pope into captivity in 1798, explained: "To tell the truth, some thirty popes had been taken prisoner or held in exile during the history of the Catholic church! But always before 1798 the enemy had been a devout Catholic who had no quarrel with Catholic teaching, only with individual popes as military opponents. What made the 1798 captivity outstanding was the fact that it came after centuries of decline in the influence of Catholicism on the people's minds. When the news had spread that the pope had been taken prisoner, not a nation in the entire world raised even a little finger to rescue him. When he died, his body was left lying around for some days before anyone buried him" (*Adventists Affirm* 12, No. 2 [summer 1998]: 3).

[5] "'Power was given unto him to continue forty and two months.' And, says the prophet, 'I saw one of his heads as it were wounded to death.' And again: 'He that leadeth into captivity shall go into captivity: he that killeth with the sword must be killed with the sword.' The forty and two months are the same as the 'time and times and the dividing of time,' three years and a half, or 1260 days, of Daniel 7—the time during which the papal power was to oppress God's people. This period, as stated in preceding chapters, began with the supremacy of the papacy, A.D. 538, and terminated in 1798. At that time the pope was made captive by the French army, the papal power received its deadly wound, and the prediction was fulfilled, 'He that leadeth into captivity shall go into captivity'" (E. G. White, *The Great Controversy*, p. 439).

[6] Daniel 7:2 represents these beasts as rising when "the four winds of the heaven strove upon the great sea." According to Revelation 17:15 water can be a symbol of "peoples, and multitudes, and nations, and tongues." Wind is a symbol of strife.

[7] "What nation of the New World was in 1798 rising into power, giving promise of strength and greatness, and attracting the attention of the world? The application of the symbol admits of

no question. One nation, and only one, meets the specifications of this prophecy; it points unmistakably to the United States of America. Again and again the thought, almost the exact words, of the sacred writer has been unconsciously employed by the orator and the historian in describing the rise and growth of this nation. The beast was seen 'coming up out of the earth'; and, according to the translators, the word here rendered 'coming up' literally signifies 'to grow or spring up as a plant.' And, as we have seen, the nation must arise in territory previously unoccupied. A prominent writer, describing the rise of the United States, speaks of *'the mystery of her coming forth from vacancy,'* and says: 'Like a *"silent seed"* we grew into empire.'—G. A. Townsend, *The New World Compared With the Old*, page 462. A European journal in 1850 spoke of the United States as a wonderful empire, which was 'emerging,' and *'amid the silence of the earth* daily adding to its power and pride.'—The *Dublin Nation*. Edward Everett, in an oration on the Pilgrim founders of this nation, said: 'Did they look for a retired spot, inoffensive for its obscurity, and safe in its remoteness, where the little church of Leyden might enjoy the freedom of conscience? Behold the *mighty regions* over which, *in peaceful conquest,* . . . they have borne the banners of the cross!'—Speech delivered at Plymouth, Massachusetts, Dec. 22, 1824, page 11" (White, *The Great Controversy,* pp. 440, 441).

[8] See John 1:29, 36; Acts 8:32; 1 Peter 1:19; Revelation 5:6, 12.

[9] White, *The Great Controversy,* p. 443.

[10] Talking about the persecution, the passage says that the United States will cause "all, both small and great, rich and poor, free and bond, to receive a mark in their right hand, or in their foreheads: and that no man might buy or sell, save he that had the mark, or the name of the beast, or the number of his name" (Revelation 13:16, 17).

[11] Anthony Lewis, "Cross and Flag," New York *Times,* Oct. 8, 1984.

[12] Sidney Blumenthal, "Christian Soldiers," *The New Yorker,* July 18, 1994, pp. 31, 32.

[13] White, *The Great Controversy,* p. 445.

[14] For the best scholarly history of the shift, see Samuele Bacchiocchi, *From Sabbath to Sunday: A Historical Investigation of the Sunday Observance in Early Christianity* (Rome: Pontifical Gregorian University, 1977). See also, Kenneth Strand, ed., *The Sabbath in Scripture and History* (Hagerstown, Md.: Review and

Herald Pub. Assn., 1982) and Clifford Goldstein, *A Pause for Peace* (Boise, Idaho: Pacific Press Pub. Assn., 1992).

[15] From the *Catholic Mirror* (Sept. 23, 1893), reprinted in *Rome's Challenge* (Washington, D.C.: Review and Herald Pub. Assn.), p. 24.

[16] Stephen Keenan, *A Doctrinal Catechism* (New York: Edward Dunigan and Brothers, 1851), p. 174.

[17] Henry Tuberville, *An Abridgment of the Christian Doctrine* (New York: Edward Dunigan and Brothers, approved 1833), p. 58.

[18] Samuel A. Cartledge, "The Sabbath—the Lord's Day," in James P. Westberry, comp., *The Lord's Day,* p. 100.

[19] One string of texts that the Protestant Reformers often used regarding the papacy was: "Let no man deceive you by any means: for that day shall not come, except there come a falling away first, and that man of sin be revealed, the son of perdition; who opposeth and exalteth himself above all that is called God, or that is worshipped; so that he as God sitteth in the temple of God, shewing himself that he is God" (2 Thessalonians 2:3, 4).

[20] Quoted in White, *The Great Controversy,* p. 448.

[21] See Isaiah 56:1, 2, 6, 7.

CHAPTER SIX

THE ORIGIN (AND PROMULGATION) OF EVIL

However important the issues surrounding the "mark of the beast," the Sabbath, and the role of the United States in prophecy may be, for many the ultimate questions go deeper. They struggle with why an all-powerful God in heaven would allow such misery on earth. Why do we find sin, suffering, and death? Why hasn't the Lord stopped evil long ago, or even before it began in the first place?

The answer is, ironically enough, that "God is love" (1 John 4:16). Love is the foundation of His divine government—and love, to be love, *must* be free. Even God Himself cannot create a forced love. God can no more command love than He can make a four-sided triangle. The moment a triangle has four sides, it's no longer a triangle; the instant love is dictated, it's no longer love. Love, by its very nature, demands free choice. Even God cannot coerce it.

One being, however, chose to pervert the freedom inherent in love. Lucifer, created by a God who does not force obedience or allegiance, decided to render neither. Scripture teaches that God created Lucifer "perfect" (Ezekiel 28:12-15). Perfection then, obviously, contained the option for evil. It must, because it was based on love, and love by its very definition includes freedom. Jealous of Christ's position as the acknowledged sovereign of heaven, Lucifer allowed pride, jealously, and hatred to gain a foothold in his heart until it climaxed in an open rebellion against God, His government, and His law.

The Lord, of course, could have obliterated Lucifer (now "Satan," a name that means "the adversary") the moment he rebelled. However, that act would only have affirmed Satan's charges that God was arbitrary, unjust, and unfair. Instead, in the presence of the holy angels and the unfallen worlds—indeed, the entire inhabited universe!—God allowed the principles that began in Satan's heart, principles of pride, self-glory, and jealousy to reach fruition. Questions about obedience, evil, and the justice of God and His law are not just earthly issues. They involve all creation, which claims a stake in the great controversy between Christ and Satan.[1]

However hard it might be for humans (in our painfully narrow, time-limited perspective) to understand, for the good of the universe, God must allow Satan's rebellion full maturity (something that hasn't happened even yet). Only then will creation—that is, the vast inhabited worlds far beyond our imagination (much less the myopic eye of the Hubble telescope)—see the results of setting aside God's law. Only then will all intelligent creatures in the cosmos fully grasp the goodness and benevolence of God's government and law in contrast to the outworking of Satan's rule. And only then, when the issues are played to completion, will God's character and His eternal law stand eternally vindicated.

After humanity's fall in Eden, Satan claimed that if the law were so holy and good that it could not be changed to meet fallen humanity, then God, to be just, had to punish the whole human race for breaking that law. For God to be just, Satan claimed (and rightly so), sin had to reap its penalty. What Satan didn't expect, however, was for God to let the punishment fall upon Christ Himself. By facing God's wrath against sin so that humanity never needed to, Christ proved not only God's justice (which did not allow sin to go unpunished) but also the changeless character of God's law, the foundation of His government of love.

Only after evil has come to its ugly conclusion at the end of the age will the whole universe witness, fully and completely, sin's true nature and results. Evil's final extermination—which, had it happened immediately when Satan rebelled, would have brought fear to the angels and dishonor to God—will instead vindicate His love and establish His honor before all intelligences, both in heaven and in earth, who will then proclaim, "Just and true are thy ways, thou King of saints" (Revelation 15:3).

But for now, as the great controversy continues to rage, Satan—unable to defeat Christ—works with all cunning, malignity, and stealth to defeat His followers instead. Only through the grace of Christ can anyone resist the deceptions and lures of the first great apostate, who has focused his enmity against the human race because they are the objects of God's love and mercy. Yet the power that Christ imparts to His followers enables them to resist Satan. "There hath no temptation taken you but such as is common to man: but God is faithful, who will not suffer you to be tempted above that ye are able; but will with the temptation also make a way to escape, that ye may be able to bear it" (1 Corinthians 10:13). Whoever abhors sin, flees it, and gains victory over its power does so only through the operation of God's Spirit. It can never be done through human effort alone.

Satan's agents constantly seek to deceive Christ's people. They attempt to sever their allegiance to Christ and thus plunge them into ruin. Humanity's foe invades every household, street, church, and public office, seeking to confuse, perplex, seduce, and ultimately destroy. White, Black, male, female, young, old, Jew, Gentile—Satan hates them all. He's an equal opportunity deceiver.

Scripture clearly teaches that angels—both fallen and unfallen—are real, and are locked in the universal battle for our souls. Though once sinless, loving beings, fallen angels have joined together with their master to dishonor God and destroy all humanity, especially those who seek to serve and honor Christ in their lives. Though Old Testament history occasionally alludes to their power and existence, the New Testament, particularly the Gospels, most forcefully reveals the reality, malignity, and power of evil angels, also known as demons.

Unquestionably Satan's most powerful and masterful

deception involves convincing people that he doesn't exist, that he's merely a concept created by ignorant ancients who developed fictitious beings in order to explain the existence of evil. It was a brilliant move! Who's going to flee or fear a nonexistent enemy? No one, which is why those who reject the reality of Satan or his demons, especially in an age of science and secular reason, are, without exception, his surest prey.

Fortunately, Jesus offers protection and deliverance. He has already defeated Satan at the cross. Christ and His angels are more powerful than Satan and all his malignant imps. Even Christ's weakest followers can find shelter, power, and hope through their Redeemer. All who in humility, faith, and repentance rely wholly on the merits of Jesus Christ and claim His promises of power will find themselves under the watch and care of One who died to redeem them and who will not allow them to fall under the tempter's dominion as long as they cling to the "captain of their salvation" (Hebrews 2:10).

Meanwhile, those who resist Christ's claims and yield to Satan will face a dreadful fate. The Lord, honoring their freedom of choice, will, however reluctantly, surrender them to Satan's total control. In fact, it's this contrast, the one between those who serve Christ and those who obey Satan fully, that will climax at the end of the age in an awesome demonstration to the entire universe of the difference between good and evil, law and lawlessness, Christ and Satan. It is a demonstration in which we all, even now, participate.

The great controversy between Christ and Satan, waged since the beginning of the world, will soon close. Satan therefore has redoubled his efforts to defeat Christ's efforts in humanity's behalf. He seeks to keep as many as possible in spiritual darkness until Christ finishes His mediation in the heavenly sanctuary and the door of mercy forever shuts.

Few things, though, scare the adversary more than those who with humility surrender themselves to God in order to know truth through His Word. Scripture exposes Satan and his ploys, which is why he does everything possible to keep people from reading the Bible. If that does not work, he leads human beings to interpret Scripture through false traditions and concepts, or destroys its authority through the presuppositions and methods of higher criticism and other philosophical presuppositions.

Satan has been especially effective through what the New Testament depicts as "science falsely so called" (1 Timothy 6:20). While the passage primarily refers to ancient philosophical and religious concepts, it also applies to modern rationalistic science. Millions who believe that modern science is the ultimate arbiter of truth have lost faith in Scripture, because current scientific theories—which are liable to change at any time—often ignore or even oppose what the Bible teaches. Accepting the authority of modern secular science, such individuals reject the clear teaching of the Word at the peril of their own souls.

Satan, an expert in epistemology, the study of knowledge, knows that everything human beings believe, whether it is secular or sacred, has room for doubt. Thus, because there is much about God, His ways, and His purposes beyond finite human understanding, Satan works with masterly skill to transform men and women into skeptics, to make them distrust God or doubt His existence.

Another of Satan's effective agencies has been professed Christians themselves. By their hatred, bigotry, and false doctrines they have turned untold millions away from belief in Christianity. G. K. Chesterton's quip—"Christianity hasn't failed; it's never been tried"—is, in many ways, sadly true.

Nevertheless, none need be deceived. Christ died for all humanity. His Holy Spirit seeks to woo all men and women into a saving relationship with Him. Those willing to know God and His truth no matter what the cost to themselves will not remain in darkness. And all those who have found truth, if they in humility, faith, and repentance reach out to the Lord through prayer and study of His Word, will never be shaken loose. The weakest soul who abides in Christ is more than a match for Satan and all the host of hell, which is why the devil works with incredible subtlety and cunning to hide himself. Only in humble reliance upon God, in faith, and in obedience to all His commandments can anyone be secure from humanity's foe.

Of all Satan's strategies to deceive humanity, his nastiest was also the first he used against human beings: the belief in the innate immortality of the soul.

"Ye shall not surely die" (Genesis 3:4) the devil told Eve in Eden—and he has been repeating his lie in one form or another ever since. Even Christianity promulgates the premise with a zeal that leaves millions vulnerable to deception, despite clear biblical texts to the contrary.

According to Jesus, the opposite of eternal life with Him is eternal *death,* not a conscious state of torment. "He that believeth on the Son," He said, "hath *everlasting life:* and he that believeth not the Son shall *not see life"* (John 3:36). "For God so loved the world," Jesus stated elsewhere, "that he gave his only begotten Son, that whosoever believeth in him should not *perish,* but have *everlasting life"* (verse 16). "Enter ye in the strait gate, for wide is the gate, and broad is the way, that leadeth to *destruction* . . . because strait is the gate, and narrow is the way, which leadeth unto *life"* (Matthew 7:13, 14).

The dichotomy Jesus presents isn't between eternal bliss in heaven and eternal torture in hell, but between eternal life and death (which He calls "destruction"). Those who don't accept Jesus, He specifically said, will "perish." They are *destroyed,* obliterated, nonexistent. Paul describes it as "everlasting destruction" (2 Thessalonians 1:9)—definitely not the same as living forever, even if in some state of constant punishment.

One of the worst fruits of the teaching called immortal soulism is the outrageously demonic doctrine of eternal torment. If the soul is inherently immortal, and if the Bible teaches a hellfire (which it does), then the only option is that a loving God in heaven will torment people billions and billions of aeons for whatever sins they committed in their flicker of earthly existence here.

For this reason Christianity—which in one

breath espouses a God of infinite mercy and pity, and in another describes the fires of hell in which millions upon millions writhe even now in horrible and unending pain—has for many people become an absurd joke. What does eternal torment say about God's character? What kind of justice does it represent? After a few hundred billion aeons burning in hell, even Hitler would finally have paid for his sins. Faced with such doctrines (though in recent years more and more Christian scholars are beginning to see their error), no wonder so many have turned away from the Scriptures. Eternal torment is what Satan, not God, would do. That's why it's Satan's doctrine, not God's.

Instead, the Bible teaches that death is a sleep, and that the dead rest in the grave until the resurrection. "There shall be a resurrection of the dead, both of the just and the unjust" (Acts 24:15). Jesus Himself stated it clearly: "The hour is coming, in which all that are in the graves shall hear his voice, and shall come forth; they that have done good, unto the resurrection of life; and they that have done evil, unto the resurrection of damnation" (John 5:28, 29).

Those redeemed by Jesus rise in the "resurrection of life," while those who have not through repentance and faith accepted the pardon that Christ freely offers, but instead purposely chose sin, rebellion, and transgression, will rise in the "resurrection of damnation." The latter will then ultimately forfeit life itself. Though punished with varying intensity and duration, "according to their works," their end will be the same: eternal destruction, what the Bible calls "the second death" (Revelation 21:8).

Such punishment is, ironically enough, for their own good. After having lived in rebellion against God here, the wicked would find the peace, purity, and perfection of heaven an eternal torment. They would welcome destruction rather than have to gaze eternally upon the face of Him who died to redeem them. If they didn't want to obey God in their short spasm on earth, why would they want to forever in heaven?

No one initially chose to live. Everyone began life without their consent. But we do have a choice when it comes to eternal life. Though Christ offers the option of eternal life, that's all that it is—an option. The final destruction of the lost will simply involve people who have elected *not* to live forever finally having their choice fulfilled—the only merciful and just thing a merciful and just God can do.

Another false concept of the belief in immortal soulism is that of consciousness in death, a teaching that presents numerous problems in light of other Bible truths.

First, if the redeemed dead are alive and conscious and can watch all the suffering and pain here on earth, heaven hardly sounds like bliss. Second, what sense does a future judgment (clearly expounded in Scripture) make if the dead immediately go to heaven or hell? If they receive their reward or punishment at death, an end-time judgment has no purpose at all. Even corrupt, earthly courts give a person a trial before punishing them. Consciousness in death makes God not only cruel but unjust.

Though some verses exist that, if taken out of the context of the entire Scripture, can appear to teach consciousness in death[2]—the Bible clearly testifies that the dead are asleep, unconscious until the resurrection.

"His breath goeth forth, he returneth to his earth; in that very day his thoughts perish" (Psalm 146:14). "The living know that they shall die: but the dead know not any thing, neither have they any more a reward; for the memory of them is forgotten. Also their love, and their hatred, and their envy, is now perished; neither have they any more a portion for ever in any thing that is done under the sun. . . . There is no work, nor device, nor knowledge, nor wisdom, in the grave, whither thou goest" (Ecclesiastes 9:5-10). "In death there is no remembrance of thee: in the grave who shall give thee thanks?" (Psalm 6:5). "The dead praise not the Lord, neither any that go down into silence" (Psalm 115:17).

Peter declared of King David, already long dead: "David is not ascended into the heavens" (Acts 2:34). If the righteous dead go directly to heaven, what happened to David? Peter's words make sense only if he's asleep in the grave, awaiting the resurrection. Paul wrote that: "If the dead rise not, then is not Christ raised: and if Christ be not raised, your faith is vain; ye are yet in your sins. Then they also which are fallen asleep in Christ are perished" (1 Corinthians 15:16-18). If the righteous dead go immediately to heaven, what is Paul talking about when he argues that if the dead rise not, our faith is in vain? Why do they need resurrection if they are already enjoying heaven? If the righteous dead go immediately to bliss, why—if there is no resurrection—would those who have "fallen asleep in Christ" perish? They should already be in heaven enjoying eternal life with Christ!

Jesus told His disciples: "I go to prepare a place for you. And if I go and prepare a place for you, I will come again, and receive you unto myself; that where I am, there ye may be also" (John 14:2, 3). What can He mean if at death the righteous ascend to heaven? Christ's words make sense only if the dead sleep in the grave until He returns to resurrect them: "The Lord himself shall descend from heaven with a shout, with the voice of the archangel, and with the trump of God: and the dead in Christ shall rise first: then we which are alive and remain shall be caught up together with them in the clouds, to meet the Lord in the air: and so shall we ever be with the Lord. Wherefore comfort one another with these words" (1 Thessalonians 4:16-18). Such passages clearly contradict the notion that the righteous dead are already enjoying eternity with Christ. Only in contrast to popular theology, which states that the dead immediately receive their reward, do Paul's words have any meaning.

The Bible clearly teaches that the dead sleep in an unconscious state until the resurrection at Christ's return—and any theology or experience that claims the contrary conflicts with the Word of God itself, the ultimate and final standard of truth.

However, because they do not understand this crucial teaching, millions find themselves sure prey to Satan's cruelest ploy: making people believe that their dead loved ones are alive in another realm.

It is a delusion so powerful, so geared to play upon the emotions, so cunning and deceptive, that only a firm trust in what the Bible says can protect anyone. Once a person accepts a conscious afterlife, he or she loses the only possible defense against this most devilish lie. Without the truth about death, how can anyone not be deceived by experiences in which the "dead" seem to return?

Satan and his angels can impersonate the dead. They reproduce the looks, the words and tone, the mannerisms and characteristics of the deceased one with such incredible accuracy that the unsuspecting victims, overwhelmed by the appearance of their dead loved ones, find themselves unwittingly duped by the cruelest of all demonic tricks.

Millions already believe that they have communicated with the dead. Popular books, movies, and TV programs promulgate Satan's lie that the dead can communicate with us. The whole New Age movement rests on this deception. Were this falsehood exposed, the New Age movement—the modern counterpart to spiritualism and the occult—would shrivel up and die.

In recent years one of the fastest-spreading manifestations of Satan's lie about immortality have been near-death experiences (NDEs). In them the "clinically dead" come back to life with fantastic accounts of existence in another realm, in which they have talked sometimes with "God" or some "Higher Power," but more often with deceased friends and relatives. The phenomenon has become so common that many doctors have documented such cases, giving them the modern imprimatur of science. Countless books about such incidents make millions believe in something that contradicts the teaching of the Word of God. The crucial question here is not the reality of the experiences—they are real—but the *interpretation* placed on them and the *conclusions* drawn. On this the destiny of millions will hang. Be it a spirit conjured up at a séance, or a well-documented NDE—these incidents are all the same. Satan deceives unsuspecting souls through his power to control any human mind not directly under the power of Christ.

Yet even without this understanding of the state of the dead, Christians should sense something amiss when those who have such experiences rarely, if ever, return promoting even the most basic biblical truths.[3] Instead they claim to have met some divine power or warm fuzzy light who rarely confronts them with their sin and need of Christ's atonement. On the contrary, they recount pleasing tales of dead loved ones who never professed Christ or followed the Bible, yet are enjoying a blissful afterlife in some happy diaphanous realm where all is joy and light. If such experiences came from God, why didn't such entities admonish those who had "died" to repent, to confess their sins, to claim the blood of Jesus as their only hope for salvation, and to live in humble obedience to God—the most generic of biblical truths? Instead, in case after case they return from "death" espousing sentimental notions of love and goodness that sound more like the teachings of New Age channelers, not someone who has met the God of Abraham, Isaac, and Jacob, the God who promises to bring all things to judgment.

"They emphasize universal love at the expense of ignoring man's depravity, sin, and the ultimate judgment that is coming," wrote Dr. Leon Green, who (though not understanding the biblical concept of the condition of death) sees through the NDE deceptions. "They deny the primacy of God and the existence of the Holy Trinity. They ignore Jesus as the salvation of the world. They reject the need for repentance and the provision of grace for all mankind."[4] These facts alone should warn any Christian—even those with wrong views about death—that such experiences do not originate from God. For many, however, the delusion is overpowering.

Indeed, as the end nears and Satan plans his final assault against God's people, his deceptions will only increase. He will use every conceivable means to keep people from crucial truths. The foundation of his greatest deception, laid in Eden with his words to Eve—"Ye shall not surely die"—now manifests itself in innumerable forms and among almost all faiths. Only those kept by the power of God through faith in His Word—*even at times in blatant disregard for what appears to the senses*—will escape the deceptions sweeping the world, deceptions that will increase with subtle fierceness until the great controversy between Christ and Satan climaxes at the end of the age.

---

[1] For a clearer picture of the interest of nonhuman intelligences in the great controversy, see Job 1 and 2.

[2] For a detailed study on this issue, see Samuele Bacchiocchi, *Immortality or Resurrection* (Berrien Springs, Mich.: Biblical Perspectives; 1997).

[3] Though not understanding the biblical truth about death, Leon Green, M.D., in his book *If I Should Wake Before I Die* (Wheaton, Ill.: Crossway Books, 1997), argues against the popular interpretation of NDEs.

[4] *Ibid.,* p. 290.

CHAPTER SEVEN

TWO-MINUTE WARNING

Viewed in the light of history and Bible prophecy, one of the most amazing trends has been the rapprochement between Roman Catholics and Protestants, particularly in the United States of America—the nation that will enforce "the mark of the beast" upon the world. Despite the clear testimony of the Bible, the Reformers, and church history, Protestants today, spiritually addicted by the lure of political power, have forgotten their history, purpose, and identity. As a result, they're being seduced back to the religious darkness that cost so much blood and pain to dispel. What are "Protestants" now protesting? Certainly not the abuses, the false gospel, and the errors that their forebears sacrificed their fortunes, families, and lives to oppose.

Time and again we read announcements proclaiming various dialogues and/or statements of "unity" among Protestant denominations and between them and Roman Catholicism. Especially in America, Protestants, eager to curry favor with the Catholics, are compromising the most fundamental of all biblical doctrines—justification by faith alone—all in order to achieve unity. In the mid-1990s, for instance, leading Protestants signed two documents—*Evangelicals and Catholics Together* and *The Gift of Salvation*—that claim that the Roman Catholic Church and evangelical Protestants are "one in Christ," that they believe in the same gospel, and thus that they should join forces in order to achieve common political goals, a fascinating event in light of the long-predicted role of America and the Papacy in prophecy.

More amazing is that the Papacy, despite some superficial changes in language and phraseology, still teaches the same doctrine of salvation by faith and works that ignited the Reformation (not to mention a host of other teachings that Protestantism has long rejected). Yet blinded by their quest for political power, as well as their ignorance of prophecy and prophetic history, Protestants are more than ever seeking unity with the Roman church.

Many fine Christians throng both the Catholic and the compromising Protestant churches. What's being criticized here isn't individuals, but a political-religious system clearly condemned in Scripture. Opposition to such a system doesn't mean bigotry against individuals any more than opposition to the Soviet Union required hostility toward individual Russians. The issue, instead, involves what the Word of God teaches about truth, salvation, and apostasy.

Since the middle of the nineteenth century a number of students of prophecy have warned not only of a resurgence of papal Christianity (Revelation 13:3), but that Protestants in the United States—putting aside their old antipathy toward "Romanism"—would be in the forefront of such a resurgence. Slowly but surely, and at times with breathtaking manifestations, the prophecy is being fulfilled. Conservative evangelicals, once loudest in denouncing Rome, now sing her praises, even if they must twist and distort the pivotal biblical truth of justification by faith to do so. Some influential American Protestants even claim that Roman Catholicism teaches the gospel according to Paul and Luther.

All this is as Satan would have it, for he knows that once such different churches unite, at least enough to gain political power, persecution against anyone who disagrees with them will inevitably follow. Satan is nothing if not consistent. If something succeeds, he will use it again—and what always succeeds is the church, united with the state, to persecute dissent.

Who murdered the prophets? Religion combined with the state. Who put to death the Messiah? Religious leaders working through civil power. And who hounded, persecuted, and killed those whose only crime was to seek to live by the teachings of the Bible? The church united with the state.

In the last days, as good and evil reach a climax in the great controversy between Christ and Satan, Satan will again use the deadly mixture of the church (Catholics and Protestants) united with the state to persecute those who refuse to *"worship* the beast and his image"—those who, in obedience to the Word, "keep the commandments of God, and the faith of Jesus" (Revelation 14:11, 12).

From the beginning of his conflict with God, Satan has always sought to overthrow His law. To accomplish his purpose he began his rebellion against the Creator. God had to expel him from heaven to the earth, where he continues his war against the law. Whether he accomplishes it by getting humanity to reject the whole law or by disobeying just one precept, the result is the same. "For whosoever shall keep the whole law, and yet offend in one point, he is guilty of all" (James 2:10). The last great conflict between truth and error, between salvation by faith alone and salvation by faith and works (which is no real salvation at all), is but the final struggle over the longstanding controversy about divine law. The world will soon enter the final struggle, a conflict between human laws and traditions and the precepts of God.

Through two great errors, the concept of an immortal human soul and the idea of Sunday sacredness, Satan is bringing Christianity completely under his control. Immortal soulism leaves Christians defenseless against the deceptions of spiritualism, the occult, and the New Age (despite the fervent denunciations of many Christians against all three), while Sunday sacredness creates a bond of sympathy between Catholics and Protestants. Sooner or later Catholics and Protestants, united through their common errors, will push the United States into enforcing Sunday worship. In contrast, those who express their love to God by keeping *all* His commandments ("This is the love of God, that we keep his commandments" [1 John 5:3]) including the seventh-day Sabbath, will find themselves denounced as enemies of law and order. Society will accuse them of causing anarchy and chaos, and of bringing God's wrath upon the world. Laws and threats will seek to supplement the lack of biblical authority for Sunday observance. Revelation has not shown ultimately how and under what exact conditions Sunday persecution will begin, but sooner or later a law or series or laws enforcing Sunday worship will emerge in America, and then spread across the world.

Meanwhile, relying wholly upon the merits of Jesus and knowing that their only hope of salvation rests in what Christ has done for them at the cross, those who love God and obey His commandments ("This is love, that we walk after his commandments" [2 John 1:6]) will face fierce opposition. Only men and women who have fortified their minds by studying the Bible will remain faithful amid such intense conflict. The burning question for them will be the same that many asked—with their lives at stake—during the reign of both pagan and papal Rome: will we follow human precepts, or the precepts of the God whose spilled blood offers us eternal life?

The world is entering the most solemn period of all history. People will decide their eternal destinies by whether they choose Christ or the doctrines and precepts of human institutions. As Jesus said, "In vain they do *worship* me, teaching for doctrines the commandments of men" (Matthew 15:9). The issue, as Jesus clearly indicated, was—and especially will be—*worship*.

All followers of Jesus, understanding the impossibility of saving themselves, must *totally* surrender themselves in body and mind to the Holy Spirit so that He can lead them into true worship and obedience. Others not yet knowing Jesus and the salvation He offers through His perfect obedience to the law (an obedience no one else can claim), yet who want to know the truth, *no matter the cost,* will find it in *Jesus Christ as revealed in the Scriptures.* When they are willing to put aside pride, preconceptions, and even the teachings of a lifetime (if need be), and in humility, prayer, repentance, and pleadings seek God's will through the Word, they will learn God's truth, no matter how painful the process.

All who stand for truth will, as these events unfold, face relentless opposition. Yet not a single individual, as long as they cling to Christ in faith and humility, will succumb to the torrent released against them. The soon-coming conflict will fulfill the words of the prophet: "The dragon was wroth with the woman, and went to make war with the remnant of her seed, which keep the commandments of God, and have the testimony of Jesus Christ" (Revelation 12:17).

For many, the warnings of the three angels' messages seem too fantastic, too far-fetched, to be believed. America, they claim, will always be what it has always been—a bastion of religious freedom. The prediction that a united church and state would bring persecution—especially over the Sabbath—appears absurd, if not impossible.

Such thinking reminds one of "Bertrand Russell's chicken." Because every morning the farmer came out to feed it, the fowl assumed every morning that the farmer's approach meant food. Then one morning the farmer came—and wrung the chicken's neck!

The past, as Russell suggested, does not guarantee the future. America's never having been a religious persecutor before doesn't mean it can't become one later. During times of great trial or stress America has, in fact, already violated fundamental rights. The saddest example has been the illegal imprisonment of Japanese-Americans during World War II. One would have to be sadly naive about the human potential for evil in order to believe that something similar can't happen again, only worse.

The United States has been lamblike *only* because nothing has angered it enough to make it speak like a dragon. Yet let something hit the beast hard enough, especially in a vulnerable spot (such as its pocketbook), and everything will change.

The biblically predicted persecution will come, and when it does it will see the three angels' messages propelled with a power unlike anything ever known before. Catholics, Protestants, secularists, even those of non-Christian religions, will take a bold stand for truth as the prophecies unfold like a play in which they have already read the script and know the lines, the acts, and the concluding scene.

As in the days of Christ, religious leaders will vehemently oppose those who, in defiance of popular teaching, worship the Lord in obedience to His commandments. With insufficient biblical evidence to bolster their claims, such false spiritual shepherds will seek the power of the state to enforce their false doctrines, in this case Sunday sacredness. When that happens, those living in obedience to God's law will have only one reply to their accusers: "Show us our error from the Word of God."

All over the world Christ's faithful followers, imbued with an outpouring of the Holy Spirit similar to what happened at Pentecost (see Acts 3:19, 20), will spread God's final message of mercy from a crucified and risen Saviour. The Holy Spirit will perform miracles, heal the sick, and manifest signs and wonders. Satan will also work with amazing deceptions, even bringing down fire from heaven (Revelation 13:13), a falsification and perversion of Elijah's confrontation with error at Mount Carmel. Thus miracles in and of themselves don't prove who's right and who's wrong—only the Word of God is the final and ultimate arbiter of truth.

To human wisdom this all now seems impossible. But that's part of the problem. To try to understand the issues with human wisdom alone is like attempting to measure the entire creation acre by acre. The great controversy between Christ and Satan goes far beyond human insight, rational thinking, and mere science and empiricism. Instead, it reaches far into the realm of the supernatural, even to the Divine, who in His infinite wisdom has revealed these crucial truths to all who will listen and, most important, obey.

"Incline your ear, and come unto me: hear, and your soul shall live; and I will make an everlasting covenant with you, even the sure mercies of David" (Isaiah 55:3).

At that time shall Michael stand up, the great prince which standeth for the children of thy people: and there shall be a time of trouble, such as never was since there was a nation even to that same time: and at that time thy people shall be delivered, every one that shall be found written in the book" (Daniel 12:1).

Scripture here points to a period when Christ's ministry in the heavenly sanctuary has ceased. God has rendered judgment "to the saints" (Daniel 7:22). Every human being capable of rational choice has decided either for or against Christ. Mercy no longer pleads for the human race. Every case has been decided. The cry now echoes from heaven: "He that is unjust, let him be unjust still: and he which is filthy, let him be filthy still: and he that is righteous, let him be righteous still: and he that is holy, let him be holy still" (Revelation 22:11). Those who have chosen Satan over Christ in the climactic battle between good and evil (also known as Armageddon) will have placed themselves completely under Satan's control. God's angels will no longer hold back strife. Instead, evil, passion, and violence will unleash themselves as never before, plunging the whole world into destruction even greater than that which overwhelmed Jerusalem in A.D. 70.

As the seventh-day Sabbath—a clear-cut and definite command of God and an overt symbol of allegiance to Him—becomes a polarizing issue throughout the world, the refusal of one group to go along with the rest of the religious world will make them objects of transnational wrath. Public opinion will blame their "impiety" for the fearsome judgments ravaging the planet. Soon a desperate human population will denounce them as worthy of death. From a human perspective alone, with the whole world against them, God's people would seem to have little hope. The truth, of course, is that they have all the hope ever possibly garnered in both heaven and earth. It's their enemies who are, indeed, without it.

The "time of trouble, such as never was" (Daniel 12:1) will soon break forth across the world. God's people will need a depth of religious experience that most don't yet possess. Now, as our great High Priest still ministers in the sanctuary above, presenting His perfect righteousness in place of our fallen human nature that Scripture compares to filthy rags, we should seek to live in trust, faith, and obedience to God. If people don't want to obey the Lord now, in relative peace and prosperity (at least in the West), how will they do it when all the forces of hell array themselves against them in terrible persecution, deception, and destruction?

And deceptive it will be. As the crowning act of the great drama between good an evil, Satan himself will impersonate Christ. In various parts of the world the archdeciever will counterfeit the description of Jesus depicted in Revelation 1:13-15 by appearing with dazzling brightness. Satan's glory will surpass anything human eyes have ever seen. The deception will be overwhelming, especially when gently and compassionately he repeats some of the same teachings the Saviour uttered, as well as heal disease as Jesus did while on earth. (Interestingly enough, all the world's great religions teach that a divine deliverer will arise in the last days. Both Christians and Muslims expect Christ to return. The Hindus await Kalki, and the Buddhists look for Maitreya. Though inspiration has not revealed this, perhaps Satan will appear among the various faiths in a manner that deceives them into believing their long-sought-for deliverer has finally arrived.) Still presenting himself as Christ, Satan will claim that he has changed the Sabbath to Sunday. Those who persist in keeping holy the seventh day, he charges, are blaspheming his name by refusing to listen to the holy angels sent to give them light and truth.

The delusion overwhelms the world, but not Christ's followers, especially when the false christ pronounces his blessing on the worshipers of the beast— the very group whom the Bible declares will face God's wrath! Also, Jesus plainly warned not only about the danger of pseudo christs but explained the true manner of His coming: "There shall arise false Christs, and false prophets, and shall shew great signs and wonders; insomuch that, if it were possible, they shall deceive the very elect. Behold, I have told you before. Wherefore if they shall say unto you, Behold, he is in the desert; go not forth: behold, he is in the secret chambers; believe it not. For as the lightning cometh out of the east, and shineth even unto the west; so shall also the coming of the Son of man be" (Matthew 24:24-27). Satan will not be able to counterfeit Christ's advent, because only the Son of God will be able to manifest Himself to the whole world at once.

Such deceptions will not sway God's commandment-keeping people. Whether in prisons or having fled to the hills, they know that God will protect them during the time of trouble. While they will not escape suffering, they will not have to endure the terrible end-time plagues poured out upon those who have rejected God: "There fell a noisome and grievous sore upon the men which had the mark of the beast, and upon them which worshipped his image" (Revelation 16:2).

In contrast, the promise for God's followers is: "Come, my people, enter thou into thy chambers, and shut thy doors about thee: hide thyself as it were for a little moment, until the indignation be overpast. For, behold, the Lord cometh out of his place to punish the inhabitants of the earth for their iniquity: the earth also shall disclose her blood, and shall no more cover her slain" (Isaiah 26:20, 21).

CHAPTER EIGHT

DELIVERANCE

When society shall finally withdraw all protection of God's people, those who honor the law of God will face a simultaneous onslaught. Thinking that they are doing God's will, the enraged masses under Satan's absolute control will seek the final solution of those who refuse to worship the beast and his image.

It is then, when unrestrained evil reaches its climax (as the onlooking universe sees where rebellion against God's law ultimately leads), that Jesus Christ, in fulfillment of His own repeated promises, finally returns. When He does, the world that we have known will forever end.

As He descends in might, majesty, and glory, heaven and earth totter and tremble. The fundamental laws of nature go berserk. Mountains shake, and the seas explode into fury. Cities crumble into ruins. "Howl ye; for the day of the Lord is at hand," the prophet said. "It shall come as a destruction from the Almighty" (Isaiah 13:6). The wicked find themselves filled with horror. "And the kings of the earth, and the great men, and the rich men, and the chief captains, and the mighty men, and every bondman, and every free man, hid themselves in the dens and in the rocks of the mountains; and said to the mountains and rocks, Fall on us, and hide us from the face of him that sitteth on the throne, and from the wrath of the Lamb: for the great day of his wrath is come; and who shall be able to stand?" (Revelation 6:15-17).

Amid the turmoil and confusion, a blazing light fills the sky—the glory of Jesus on a dazzling white cloud of unfallen angels. At His first advent He had been the man of sorrows. Now He returns in His full glory. "And he hath on his vesture and on his thigh a name written, KING OF KINGS, and LORD OF LORDS" (Revelation 19:16). No mind can begin to grasp the awesomeness of Christ's second advent.

Then, in an act that defies the world's most profound wisdom, that mocks the world's greatest philosophers, that exposes the weaknesses and limits of all the world's science, Christ—the great Life-giver—shouts with a voice that penetrates every part of the earth: "Awake, awake, awake, ye that sleep in the dust, and arise!" (see Ephesians 5:14). All over the planet the righteous dead—even those in the cold depths of the sea or locked in the rocks of the earth—instantly spring forth to immortality and perfection. The resurrected ones, along with those faithful ones alive when Jesus returns—a people who "in a moment, in the twinkling of an eye" (1 Corinthians 15:52) have received immortality—soar from our ruined earth into a whole new existence: "We which are alive and remain unto the coming of the Lord shall not prevent them which are asleep. For the Lord himself shall descend from heaven with a shout, with the voice of the archangel, and with the trump of God: and the dead in Christ shall rise first: then we which are alive and remain shall be caught up together with them in the clouds, to meet the Lord in the air: and so shall we ever be with the Lord" (1 Thessalonians 4:15-17).

Together all the redeemed from every age, nation, and tongue begin the most fantastic of voyages—to the City of God, the New Jerusalem, the crown jewel of heaven itself. There, as the saved gather in this heavenly city, Jesus' prayer—"I will that they also, whom thou hast given me, be with me where I am" (John 17:24)—will at last be answered. There, with unutterable love, Jesus welcomes those bought with the unmatchable price of His blood. And there all who have endured shame and humiliation for Christ's sake, who have experienced disappointment and woe for Christ's sake, who have denied self and loved others for Christ's sake will receive their reward. All realize that only the infinite sacrifice made in their behalf has made them worthy of heaven.

Pain, weeping, and sorrow will have vanished forever. Christ Himself has wiped away every tear. Grief—and every cause of it—has been removed, never to return. In total joy the redeemed lift their voices in praise, shouting: "Salvation to our God which sitteth on the throne, and unto the Lamb." The watching inhabitants of heaven respond: "Amen: Blessing, and glory, and wisdom, and thanksgiving, and honour, and power, and might, be unto our God for ever and ever" (Revelation 7:10, 12).

Even in the full light of God's presence, the incredible mystery—that the One who created and sustains all the universe should take on human flesh and bear Himself the guilt and shame and penalty of the sin of a lost world until it broke His heart and crushed out His life—will forever stir the excitement and wonder of all intelligent creation. "Worthy, worthy is the Lamb that was slain, and hath redeemed us to God by his own most precious blood!" they shout in praise of the One who humiliated Himself in order that they may be saved and glorified.

As heaven reveals more and more of the plan of salvation, the redeemed will see that God could save us only through the sacrifice of His Son. Yet the compensation for that sacrifice—the earth peopled with ransomed beings, holy, happy, sinless, and immortal—was worth it for Jesus, who, as Scripture says, "shall see of the travail of his soul, and shall be satisfied . . . for he shall bear their iniquities" (Isaiah 53:11).

The Lord cometh out of his place to punish the inhabitants of the earth for their iniquity: the earth also shall disclose her blood, and shall no more cover her slain" (Isaiah 26:21). "And the slain of the Lord shall be at that day from one end of the earth even unto the other end of the earth: they shall not be lamented, neither gathered, nor buried; they shall be dung upon the ground" (Jeremiah 25:33).

The brightness of Jesus' return destroys the wicked. Then, while the saved are enjoying the bliss of the heavenly city, the earth is left ruined, desolate, empty.

For 1,000 years our dead planet is the wasteland prison of Satan and his angels. John the revelator, after describing the Second Coming and the death of the lost, writes: "I saw an angel come down from heaven, having the key of the bottomless pit and a great chain in his hand. And he laid hold on the dragon, that old serpent, which is the Devil, and Satan, and bound him a thousand years, and cast him into the bottomless pit, and shut him up, and set a seal upon him, that he should deceive the nations no more, till the thousand years should be fulfilled: and after that he must be loosed a little season" (Revelation 20:1-3). The Greek word for "bottomless pit" is the same word used in the Greek translation of the Old Testament for the "deep" of Genesis 1, a depiction of the earth in its chaotic condition before the Lord created life here. Prophecy teaches that this chaos will return, at least partially. "I beheld the earth, and, lo, it was without form, and void; and the heavens, and they had no light. I beheld the mountains, and, lo, they trembled, and all the hills moved lightly. I beheld, and, lo, there was no man, and all the birds of the heavens were fled. I beheld, and, lo, the fruitful place was a wilderness, and all the cities thereof were broken down at the presence of the Lord, and by his fierce anger" (Jeremiah 4:23-26).

For 1,000 years, the millennium, Satan will remain banished amid these ruins, where he will be left to contemplate the terrible results of his rebellion. Limited to the earth, he will not have access to the unfallen worlds that he has tempted and annoyed in the past. With the wicked all dead and out of his reach and control, he will wander aimlessly amid the scars of our desolate planet with none to deceive, torment, or kill.

In contrast, during the millennium—which separates the first and second resurrections—the redeemed in heaven will review the judgment of the lost. The heavenly records will answer many of the questions that now seem so unanswerable. The pains, the disappointments, the tragedies, the deaths, the seemingly senseless and meaningless sufferings that have ravaged human existence, will at last all receive definitive answers. It will be a thousand years' worth of answers that will shed unending light upon what's now only darkness and despair. The apostle Paul wrote specifically of this period: "Judge nothing before the time, until the Lord come, who both will bring to light the hidden things of darkness, and will make manifest the counsels of the hearts: and then shall every man have praise of God" (1 Corinthians 4:5). The saved will reign with Christ: "They shall be priests of God and of Christ, and shall reign with him a thousand years" (Revelation 20:6). It is then that, as foretold by Paul, "the saints shall judge the world" (1 Corinthians 6:2). In unison with Jesus, the redeemed will review all the deeds of the lost, even the hidden and secret things, and according to their deeds the lost will be judged. Christ and His people will judge even Satan and his angels. "Know ye not that we shall judge angels?" (verse 3).

At the close of the millennium the second resurrection will take place as the lost rise to answer for their sins. "The rest of the dead lived not again until the thousand years were finished" (Revelation 20:5). It is then, and only then, that hell becomes a reality—only a hell hotter, yet infinitely more merciful, than the one portrayed by the doctrine of eternal torment. Once and for all, justice, so alien to the human experience now, will finally and flawlessly be executed.

After the 1,000 years Christ returns to the earth again—this time with His people clothed in immortality. Descending in awesome majesty, Jesus raises the unredeemed dead. The cold ground and turbulent seas finally expel them to meet their Maker. Next the New Jerusalem descends to the Mount of Olives (Zechariah 14:4, 5, 9). Jesus, the saved, and the holy angels enter its lofty gates.

Satan, seeing the vast throng of beings who had once been under his control, prepares one last desperate assault against Christ and His followers. Hiding his true identity, he assures the risen multitude that he is their redeemer, that he raised them, and that he can lead them into a victorious battle for the Holy City, which he claims belongs rightfully to them. The masses, having followed Satan in their first life, find themselves easily swayed by him in the next. With all the genius, cunning, and power of some of the world's greatest scientists, thinkers, and military leaders, an army bigger, vaster, and more powerful than any ever created before in human history prepares to attack the New Jerusalem.

As this endless sea of flesh and passion advances, Christ appears—sitting above the Holy City upon His throne in a glory and majesty beyond words. Vested with supreme authority and power, Jesus pronounces judgment upon those outside the city, those who have openly transgressed His law and refused His grace: "I saw a great white throne, and him that sat on it, from whose face the earth and heaven fled away; and there was found no place for them. And I saw the dead, small and great, stand before God; and the books were opened: and another book was opened, which is the book of life: and the dead were judged out of those things which were written in the books, according to their works" (Revelation 20:11, 12).

As the record books open, every individual in the vast throng becomes painfully aware of his or her own sin, as if every evil deed burns in scarlet letters of fire that sear their souls. Suddenly, across the sky, like a giant video screen, the plan of salvation plays itself out before them, from Adam's fall to Christ's humiliation on the cross. None can look away. From Satan on down all see their wickedness, the evil they have cultivated, and the sins they thought were long ago hidden and forgotten. In the light of the cross, all finally recognize themselves for what they really are, because now they have the ultimate standard of truth and righteousness to contrast against their own hypocrisy, sensuality, greed, jealousy, hatred, violence, and malice. They have no more excuses, no more justifications, no more deceptions. All stand arraigned at the heavenly bar on the charge of high treason against God's law. But they have none to plead their case, none to stand as their substitute and advocate when God pronounces the sentence of eternal death on them—a sentence that each one is forced by overwhelming evidence to admit is just and righteous and fair. All, in fact, acknowledge that their exclusion from heaven is the only thing that God can possibly do.

Even Satan himself, the archrebel, the first great apostate, admits the fallacy of his ways in contrast to the mercy and love of God. With no more excuses, no more accusations, no more lies, he bows and confesses the justice of the sentence imposed upon him. Heaven, he knows, would be hell for him as well.

"Every question of truth and error in the long-standing controversy has now been made plain. The results of rebellion, the fruits of setting aside the divine statutes, have been laid open to the view of all created intelligences. The working out of Satan's rule in contrast with the government of God has been presented to the whole universe. Satan's own works have condemned him. God's wisdom, His justice, and His goodness stand fully vindicated. It is seen that all His dealings in the great controversy have been conducted with respect to the eternal good of His people and the good of all the worlds that He has created. 'All thy works shall praise thee, O Lord; and thy saints shall bless thee.' Psalm 145:10. The history of sin will stand to all eternity as a witness that with the existence of God's law is bound up the happiness of all the beings He has created. With all the facts of the great controversy in view, the whole universe, both loyal and rebellious, with one accord declare: 'Just and true are thy ways, thou King of saints.'"[1]

Nevertheless, despite his admission, Satan's spirit of rebellion doesn't end. Rushing amid the throng, he inspires them to attack the city. But among those whom he once led so easily, none now acknowledge his supremacy. In fact, seeing that their case is hopeless and that they can't prevail against God, they turn against Satan himself with demonic fury.

At that moment God unleashes the final, terrible punishment that He never meant for humans but only for the devil and his angels. "Upon the wicked he shall rain snares, fire and brimstone, and an horrible tempest: this shall be the portion of their cup" (Psalm 11:6). Fire blazes down from God out of heaven. And though it does not touch the Holy City and the saints, it consumes the wicked, some in an instant, some longer—but all punished "according to their deeds" (Psalm 28:4). And though suffering long after all the destruction of the others, the prince of darkness is himself finally obliterated.

As the fire rages, the planet's surface becomes one molten mass as the elements melt (2 Peter 3:10). The fire that destroys sin, sinners, and Satan also cleanses, completely incinerating all traces of a fallen world and preparing it to be recreated.

Only one reminder of sin remains after the fires die and the melted stone and metal cool. Upon His wounded head, upon His side, His hands and feet, Christ—now crowned as king—will forever bear the scars of His crucifixion as the eternal symbol of the cost of human redemption.

And I saw a new heaven and a new earth: for the first heaven and the first earth were passed away; and there was no more sea" (Revelation 21:1).

God's original purpose for humanity's creation now stands fulfilled. The old earth, purged in the fires of hell, becomes the new earth, recreated in all its former beauty until it's good and glorious enough to be the eternal home of Christ's ransomed. All that had been lost through rebellion and disobedience God has forever restored.

Our human minds—darkened, limited, narrow— now can't begin to comprehend this new existence. "Eye hath not seen, nor ear heard, neither have entered into the heart of man, the things which God hath prepared for them that love him" (1 Corinthians 2:9). Our experience (eye and ear) and reason (the heart) are as inadequate for conveying to us God's ultimate promise as they are for understanding the borders of the universe or for hearing the hum of electrons. Even with the great light that inspiration provides, we see only through a glass darkly.

"The wolf also shall dwell with the lamb, and the leopard shall lie down with the kid; . . . a little child shall lead them" (Isaiah 11:6). "There shall be no more death, neither sorrow, nor crying, . . . for the former things are passed away" (Revelation 21:4). At the center of the glorified new earth looms the New Jerusalem, whose "light was like unto a stone most precious, even like a jasper stone, clear as crystal; and had a wall great and high, and had twelve gates, and at the gates twelve angels, and names written thereon, which are the names of the twelve tribes of the children of Israel. . . . And the city was pure gold, like unto clear glass. . . . And I saw no temple therein: for the Lord God Almighty and the Lamb are the temple of it. And the city had no need of the sun, neither of the moon, to shine in it: for the glory of God did lighten it, and the Lamb is the light thereof. And the nations of them which are saved shall walk in the light of it: and the kings of the earth do bring their glory and honour into it. And the gates of it shall not be shut at all by day: for there shall be no night there" (Revelation 21:11-25).

In this new world, radically different from all that we have ever experienced or imagined, the redeemed will develop every faculty, increase every potential. They will be able to carry out the grandest desires, realize the highest ambitions. The loves and sympathies and passions that God Himself planted in us will have their fullest expression, unhindered by the limits of sin and death that now hold us in check.

There, in the joys of a world without the curse of the Fall, the redeemed will be able to study all the treasures of the universe as they never again face a tempter or the wiles of sin. With every question fully answered, with the character of God fully vindicated, those bought with His blood and freed from the mental and physical fetters of mortality will travel the universe and share the joy and wisdom of unfallen beings as all bask in the wondrous love of their God. With undimmed vision they will gaze upon creation and see in every created thing a reflection of the love and majesty of the Creator.

As eternity continues, knowledge will increase, and with knowledge will come an endlessly growing love, respect, and admiration for God. As Jesus reveals to them all that He did to redeem them, climaxing in the amazing sacrifice of Calvary—which alone granted them the privilege of eternal life—the ransomed will with astonishment, wonder, and love praise their God and Redeemer. Hard as it might seem now, as we're so helplessly trapped by the time and space limitations of our existence here, we will not dwell on the pain, suffering, and woe that we once endured—not in the light, the glory, and the joy that will be ours because of Christ and His death on the cross.

"The great controversy is ended. Sin and sinners are no more. The entire universe is clean. One pulse of harmony and gladness beats through the vast creation. From Him who created all, flow life and light and gladness, throughout the realms of illimitable space. From the minutest atom to the greatest world, all things, animate and inanimate, in their unshadowed beauty and perfect joy, declare that God is love."[2]

Beautiful things, indeed . . .

---

[1] E. G. White, *The Great Controversy*, p. 670, 671.
[2] *Ibid.*, p. 678.